Sermons For Advent/Christmas/Epiphany Based On First Lesson Texts For Cycle C

Where Is God In All This?

Tony Everett

CSS Publishing Company, Inc., Lima, Ohio

SERMONS FOR ADVENT/CHRISTMAS/EPIPHANY BASED ON FIRST LESSON TEXTS FOR CYCLE C: WHERE IS GOD IN ALL THIS?

Copyright © 1997 by
CSS Publishing Company, Inc.
Lima, Ohio

All rights reserved. No part of this publication may be reproduced in any manner whatsoever without the prior permission of the publisher, except in the case of brief quotations embodied in critical articles and reviews. Inquiries should be addressed to: Permissions, CSS Publishing Company, Inc., P.O. Box 4503, Lima, Ohio 45802-4503.

Some scripture quotations are from the *New Revised Standard Version of the Bible*, copyright 1989 by the Division of Christian Education of the National Council of the Churches of Christ in the USA. Used by permission.

Some scripture quotations are from the *Revised Standard Version of the Bible*, copyrighted 1946, 1952 ©, 1971, 1973, by the Division of Christian Education of the National Council of the Churches of Christ in the USA. Used by permission.

Library of Congress Cataloging-in-Publication Data

Everett, Daryl S.
   Sermons for Advent/Christmas/Epiphany based on first lesson texts for cycle C : where is God in all this? / Daryl S. "Tony" Everett.
     p.   cm.
   ISBN 0-7880-1028-X (pbk.)
   1. Advent sermons. 2. Christmas sermons. 3. Epiphany season — Sermons. 4. Bible. O.T. — Sermons. 5. Sermons, American. 6. Common lectionary (1992)   I. Title.
BV4254.5.E94   1997
252'.61— dc21   96-46511
                                                                                  CIP

This book is available in the following formats, listed by ISBN:
   0-7880-1028-X Book
   0-7880-1071-9 Mac
   0-7880-1072-7 IBM 3 1/2
   0-7880-1073-5 Sermon Prep

PRINTED IN U.S.A.

To Judy,
My Best Friend and Life Partner

and

To Lisa, Lori and Dan,
Our children and now our colleagues
in serving all God's children

Whose love and support forever illumine
Where God Is In All This

Editor's Note Regarding The Lectionary

During the past two decades there has been an attempt to move in the direction of a uniform lectionary among various Protestant denominations.

Preaching on the same scripture lessons every Sunday is a step in the right direction of uniting Christians of many faiths. If we are reading the same scriptures together, we may also begin to accomplish other achievements. Our efforts will be strengthened through our unity.

Beginning with Advent 1995 The Evangelical Lutheran Church in America dropped its own lectionary schedule and adopted the Revised Common Lectionary.

Reflecting this change, resources published by CSS Publishing Company put their major emphasis on the Revised Common Lectionary texts for the church year.

Acknowledgments

I am deeply grateful to several persons for their support and insights during the preparation of these sermons.

Thomas E. Ridenhour, Academic Dean and Professor of Homiletics, has provided both encouragement and humor during the frequent bleak and empty times. His advice has been clear and precise: Listen to the Word of the Lord — Dabar Adonai — in the text. Proclaim the Good News of Jesus Christ;

Lamontte M. Luker, Associate Professor Hebrew Scriptures, has supplied many helpful suggestions regarding translation and exegesis of difficult passages;

H. Frederick Reisz, President of Lutheran Theological Southern Seminary, offered to write the Foreword to this book even before reading it. His ministry within this community continues to inspire and model what it means to walk with Christ on the journey of faith;

Students and former parishioners have continued to challenge me to ask the "Where-Is-God-In-All-This?" question and to point me in new directions when a clear answer is not really forthcoming;

Joan Long, Faculty Secretary, has labored tirelessly and faithfully in typing and revising the manuscript.

I am indebted to the entire community of believers at Lutheran Theological Southern Seminary for demonstrating continuously what it means to be "Walking Wet" among the baptized people of God.

Tony S. Everett

Table Of Contents

Foreword	9
Introduction	11
Advent 1 Why Did Pastor Hypnotize Jenny? Jeremiah 33:14-16	15
Advent 2 Advent Of Angels Malachi 3:1-4	19
Advent 3 Anticipation Proclamation Zephaniah 3:14-20	23
Advent 4 Tiny Town: Promised Power Micah 5:2-5a	27
Christmas Eve/Day Unexpected Joy; Undeserved Gift Isaiah 9:2-7	31
Christmas 1 Gifts: Rejected And Exchanged, Accepted And Shared 1 Samuel 2:18-20, 26	35
Christmas 2 An Awesome Homecoming Jeremiah 31:7-14	41
Epiphany Reach For The Light Isaiah 60:1-6	45

Baptism Of The Lord   49
    Named And Claimed
    Isaiah 43:1-7

Epiphany 2   53
    New Name, New Status
    Isaiah 62:1-5

Epiphany 3   57
    Anything But Trivial
    Nehemiah 8:1-3, 5-6, 8-10

Epiphany 4   63
    Dabar Adonai
    Jeremiah 1:4-10

Epiphany 5   67
    Seeing With New Eyes
    Isaiah 6:1-8 (9-13)

Epiphany 6   73
    Roots Near The River
    Jeremiah 17:5-10

Epiphany 7   77
    Who's In Charge Here, Anyway?
    Genesis 45:3-11, 15

The Transfiguration Of The Lord   83
(Last Sunday After The Epiphany)
    Looking Back; Moving Forward
    Exodus 34:29-35

Foreword

Dr. Tony S. Everett provides us with a series of life-related sermons on the Old Testament lessons for Sundays in the Advent, Christmas, and Epiphany seasons. These lessons from the Hebrew scriptures are given breath to be living words for Christian communities. The sermons are biblically and theologically responsible, not sacrificing the message for relevance. These sermons are also immediately relevant to daily experience, not sacrificing existential clarity for scholarly obscurantism. If I were in the pew, I would be drawn to listen to this preacher, and his examples and words would follow me into the week!

These sermons are contextual without being narrow. They open windows onto living in many times and many places. They are filled with natural illustrations drawn from the careful listening of a pastor-counselor. The lives of the people of God are evident. There is enough humor in the midst to lighten the load but never to throw it aside. The sermons move into a depth of biblical interpretation and then run out to apply that meaning in our lives. Thus listeners will become hearers of the Word.

The sermons often begin with an opening paragraph designed to connect with the hearer. Then the biblical text is explicated in clear, unadorned language. All the exegetical work has evidently been done, but it is not put on display to "justify" the scholarly credentials of the preacher. The style is more conversational and natural. Following the biblical explication immediately that Word is illustrated with one or more examples from contemporary life which absolutely ring true. These illustrations are proclamations of possibilities for the people of God. I found myself scrutinizing my own living, envisioning other possibilities. The implications for Christians of these Hebrew texts are clarified in explicitly Christ-related theological statements. At the conclusion of each sermon, the text and our lives are brought together in the last paragraph so that we take with us inspiration, wisdom, and callings as the people of Christ. It is apparent "where God is in all of this."

I appreciate how the Hebrew scriptures are given their integrity in these sermons. Then the explicitly Christian theological reflection appears, often later in the sermon. Here Christ appears in the midst as he does in our lives, and Christ is at the end as he surely and fully will be. The form of the sermons themselves is that theological proclamation.

The first sentence of this sermon series is, "It was a particularly exciting moment in the worship service," and the last sentence of the book is, "Christ, our eternal resource, walks with us in our journey, on the way." These sermons point to the excitement of the Spirit stirring in these seasons of the church year, and they awake us to Christ leading us forward into life.

    The Rev. Dr. H. Frederick Reisz, Jr.
    President, Lutheran Theological Southern Seminary
    Columbia, South Carolina

Introduction

Baseball Hall of Fame catcher Yogi Berra once remarked, "When you come to a crossroads, take it."

Throughout history the people of God have found themselves at one confusing crossroads after another. Each generation has approached and has made unsuccessful attempts to define and resolve its own particular crises exclusively within a secular framework.

Military and political definitions and solutions ultimately resulted in disaster and destruction. Incorporating pagan values and practices into the covenant demands of the Lord inevitably led to corruption and apathy.

Our generation of God's baptized people has learned little from the mistakes of our foreparents. We, too, are at a crossroads. How we define the crises and challenges of our time shapes the path we take to resolve them.

I have come to understand the real crossroads faced by the Church today as biblical, not organizational; theological, not financial; spiritual, not numerical. The real crisis we face in the Church today is one of faithful belief and mission instead of psychological relief and accommodation.

The Old Testament lessons for the Seasons of Advent, Christmas, and Epiphany call us to define our crises in the language of identity. Who and Whose are we anyway? To what kind of community do we really belong? What difference does it make? What is God calling us to be and to do?

These exciting narratives are set in contexts of confusion and crisis. Each lesson presents a clear and precise Word of the Lord to address a specific situation. They challenge us to be open to rediscover the loving will of God within our own personal and congregational crossroads.

Inevitably we attempt to shape our responses according to the language and expectations of our culture.

It is easy for us to seek "quick-fix" solutions to challenges of declining attendance, shrinking income and disappearing volunteers. We search in futility for simple techniques that promise the moon. Unfortunately, we soon discover that these gimmicks are like the River Platte in Nebraska; a mile wide, but only an inch deep. Invariably such feeble solutions flash for a brief time, then crash in chaos.

The title of this book has its origin in years of mutual ministry with persons and congregations wrestling with significant crisis experiences.

Fortunately in times like this, someone usually asks the crucial and basic question of our identity as the baptized people of God: Where Is God In All This? That question quickly expands our vision and challenges our hasty conclusions; that question calls us back to the center of life and the core of meaning: the reality of God's forgiving love in Jesus Christ. The Old Testament lessons for these seasons point us to that promised reality.

God needs to be the subject of more verbs as we encounter the crossroads of life. WIGIAT (Where Is God In All This) has been placed on banners and bumper stickers and notebooks and newsprint in many homes and congregations. It serves as a reminder that our identity is rooted and grounded in the Living Word of the Lord, Jesus Christ. That Word walks with us through any crisis that life may bring.

It is the preaching task to ask the WIGIAT question, and to engage the hearers in an encounter with the biblical text. The preacher proclaims the Word of the Lord in a particular context.

I must confess that preparing written sermons to be read by persons with whom I have no prior relationship was a daunting task, even more formidable than I had first imagined. On the one hand, issues that grasped the attention and evoked the fears of people in South Carolina in 1996 may have little meaning for any of you as you read this. So, strike "contemporary" illustrations. On the other hand, this project has forced me to focus first and last on the text itself, the Word of God for our time and for *all* times. I now have a glimpse into what Jacob must have experienced as he wrestled with a representative of the Lord at Peniel (Genesis 32:24f).

I invite you, also, to wrestle with these texts as you strive to discern Where-Is-God-In-All-This? for you and for the particular baptized children of God with whom you dwell.

                Tony S. Everett
                Lutheran Theological Southern Seminary
                Columbia, South Carolina
                August, 1996

Why Did Pastor Hypnotize Jenny?

Advent 1 *Jeremiah 33:14-16*

It was a particularly exciting moment in the worship service. Pastor Steve stepped to the front of the chancel and in a powerful voice announced, "It's time for Jenny's baptism!" He walked quickly to the baptismal font where Jenny waited, clinging to her father's neck, eyes wide open in wonder. All the children in the sanctuary, as was their custom, rushed to the font. They gathered around Jenny, her parents and godparents. Standing on tiptoe, they struggled to see the smiling faces and to hear the splashing water. Jenny was about to be named "Child of God" and become a member of God's own family. Holding Jenny in his arms, Pastor Steve poured the water on her tiny head, loudly proclaiming, "Jenny, I baptize you in the name of the Father and of the Son and of the Holy Spirit. Amen." Well, all this was too much for little Gary who began to shout, "Why did Pastor hypnotize Jenny? Why did Pastor hypnotize Jenny?"

Well, the word wasn't quite precise, Gary, but you certainly caught the excitement of the sacrament. You'll grow in wisdom, knowledge, and understanding as you remain in God's family. You were on target about something though. Sometimes it appears as if we Christians face the world's problems and challenges as if we really are in a helpless and hopeless hypnotic trance.

As we begin this Advent Season just a few short years from the twenty-first century, we are painfully aware of a growing sense of disillusionment in our society. Basic values are questioned. Optimism for the future is rare. Cynicism and pessimism abound. A persistent skepticism exists regarding personal, political, and corporate integrity. Three years ago the National Opinion Research Center released data stating that approximately two thirds of Americans believe that most people cannot be trusted. For many, the Church no longer is a priority as a source of meaning, commitment, and direction in life. The reality of God's transforming love in Jesus Christ is often perceived, at best, as one option among many paths to success and salvation. Where is God in all this?

Disillusionment, despair, doubt, and skepticism also describe the context of today's text in Jeremiah 33:14-16. Jeremiah first addressed these words to a Jewish population devastated by war and exiled by the Babylonian army (see Jeremiah 23:5-6). Then he repeated them again in our text to the Jews who had joyously returned to the homeland after a fifty-year captivity.

However, soon their joy turned into discouragement. The Temple in Jerusalem was still in ruins. Progress on rebuilding city walls was minimal. Some doubted that their return actually was the Lord's doing. Some were ready to renounce their religious heritage and give allegiance to a variety of differing pagan practices.

Sound familiar? The Lord spoke to the discouraged inhabitants of Jerusalem in the sixth century B.C., and to the Jewish exiles in Babylonia fifty years before. The Lord also speaks to us today on this first Sunday of Advent during the last years of the twentieth century:

> *Behold, the days are coming, says the Lord, when I will fulfill the promise I made to the house of Israel and the house of Judah. In those days and at that time I will cause a righteous Branch to spring forth for David; and he shall execute justice and righteousness in the land. In those days Judah will be saved and Jerusalem will dwell securely. And this is the name by which it will be called: "Yahweh Sidquenu" (The Lord is our righteousness).*

Here is God in action. Here is a promise of comfort and hope to those who are discouraged. Here is an admonition to remain faithful to those who are ready to give up. And, best of all, here is a promise that the Lord has kept, in Jesus, Son of God, the Christ.

We are beginning the Advent Season, in which we are reminded again, and again: "The days are here, the promise has been fulfilled." The righteous branch of David's line has come, is coming, and will come again. Yahweh Sidquenu! the Lord is indeed our righteousness.

Our righteousness, our right relationship with God, does not depend on our own action. Our right relationship with God does not depend on planning a wonderful Christmas program, preparing a magnificent meal, singing a super anthem, giving the "perfect" gift, or even on designing a prize-winning outdoor lighting system. Our relationship with God depends solely on the truly perfect gift of love that God has already given, God's only begotten son, Jesus Christ.

We are well aware that our own efforts all too often end in discouragement. Expecting perfection usually results in experiencing rejection. The weeks before Christmas bring us to the same place again and again. Everything will be all right if only they would ... if only I could ... if only God would....

If only they would rebuild the Temple; if only they would work harder on the city walls; if only God would take charge.

Perhaps similar thoughts are whirling around in your minds as you begin this season of preparation for the birth of the Christ child. Many people have already begun the countdown to Christmas. Calendars are already jammed with congregation celebrations and social events. It seems as if there aren't enough hours in each day to accomplish the countless tasks that loom ahead during the next few weeks. Our minds spin out of control as we plan for happiness but anticipate frustration. If only God would take charge.

A neighbor tells this story. Her two small sons came bursting into the house, shouting that their little sister had fallen into the pond at the back of their property.

Being an experienced mother, she had learned to ask questions before going into a full-blown panic. "Then what happened?" she asked.

"We tried giving her mouth-to-mouth recessitation," her oldest son replied. "Yeah," said the younger boy, "but she kept getting up and running away!"

This is precisely what happens when we try to be in complete charge of our own lives. Our anticipations and expectations "keep getting up and running away" from us, no matter how much we try to control them. Our desperate plans for the "ideal holiday season" rarely bring the happiness and satisfaction we had intended. Instead, the results inevitably feel more like emptiness and frustration. Today is the First Sunday of Advent, not the first day of a reckless countdown of shopping days until Christmas.

What preparations for the coming Christ child are happening in the depth of your soul? How much time and energy are you giving to the trimmings and frills of Christmas? How does that compare with the time and energy you are investing in beginning and continuing a right relationship with God?

The days have come.
The promise has been fulfilled.
A righteous branch — Jesus the Christ
Has Come, is coming,
And will come again.

No, Gary, Jenny was not hypnotized. She was baptized, bathed in the living water of the Word of God. And so were you. So were we. Just as the Hebrews in Jeremiah's day, we might act as if we are hypnotized by all the discouraging and disappointing happenings around us and within us. Nevertheless, Gary, you have reminded us that we are baptized, we are claimed by God, and we are named children of the Heavenly Father, forever. The Lord is our righteousness. The days are here. The promise has been fulfilled.

Christ has come! Christ is coming! Christ will come again!

Advent
Of Angels

Advent 2 *Malachi 3:1-4*

A seminary professor has said that there have been more books about angels produced during the past five years than in the previous 150. In our sometimes chaotic and impersonal society we have a deep yearning to be protected, loved, and guided. When we experience life's uncertainties and challenges we need a messenger from God; we need an angel to help us overcome adversity, to guide us through troubled times, to love us when we are most vulnerable, and to correct us when we stray from God's way.

And that's what God promises in our text today. The title of the last book in the Old Testament, "Malachi," is obtained from verse 1. "Behold, I send 'my messenger' (*Malachi* in Hebrew) to prepare the way before me." *Malak* is the Hebrew word for "angel." At the time of our text, the fifth century B.C., an angel was not necessarily thought of exclusively as a spiritual being from another plane of existence. (This is a prevailing view in earlier biblical writings and in current popular books.) During the fifth century B.C., an angel, Malak, was often understood to be a flesh and blood human being who brought a message from God. An angel was an envoy sent by God to prepare the ears and the hearts of the people to hear God's will.

And the folks during the time of our text surely needed to hear and to receive the will of the Lord. Elsewhere in Malachi we are told of conditions during the period about sixty years after the return to Jerusalem from exile in Babylonia. Temple services were so long and superficial that even the priests were bored and becoming lax in the performance of their duties (1:6-15). Many people were murmuring that serving the Lord was meaningless. God seemed to be indifferent to what was fair and, indeed, was not a God of justice at all (2:17 and 3:13-15). Adultery was commonplace. Lying under oath was a frequent experience in the courts. The poor were oppressed and laborers were cheated by their employers. Hospitality to the stranger was rare. Magicians and sorcerers were consulted more than the Lord (3:5).

Wow! These folks certainly needed an angel — an envoy from the Lord!

And so do we. Who is there to say that similar practices do not occur even now, even among folks who should know better? Sin abounds. Who is to say that we, too, don't need a messenger from the Lord?

God has sent many angels to us as prophets, psalmists, and apostles. Their message is available in every chapter in the Bible. God still sends angels to us in the form of baptized sisters and brothers in our congregations, as friends and family members, or even as strangers. The angels God sends to us offer wisdom and guidance, support and love. The angels God sends to us prepare our ears to hear and our hearts to receive the Advent message of power and joy: Christ has come. Christ is coming. Christ will come again.

The problem is, too often we simply don't hear The Word in the "words" of the messenger. We don't recognize the presence of the Spirit in the face of the messengers. We simply aren't prepared.

There is an old story that portrays what this is like.

A devout Christian was living with his family in an area frequently inundated by flood waters. One day, after hours of relentless rain, an evacuation of the area was ordered. The man's wife and children were preparing to leave and urged him to come along. He refused, saying, "God will send an angel to rescue me."

Soon the flooding started and his neighbors slogged through knee-deep water to beg him to evacuate. "God will send an angel to rescue me," he steadfastly replied. By this time the man was at his second story window, greeting police officers who had come by in a motorboat to rescue him. "God will send an angel to rescue me," he said. Finally, clinging to the top of his chimney to keep from being swept away by the raging waters, the man gave the same response to a National Guard officer in a helicopter.

Soon the man found himself face-to-face with the Lord, and complained, "Why didn't you send your messenger to rescue me?" The Lord replied, "I sent you your family, your neighbors, a motorboat, and a helicopter, and you wouldn't listen."

Where is God in all this?

You see, God does send us angels, messengers/envoys of admonition, love and deliverance to support us and admonish us. God does send angels to help us experience anew God's forgiving, amazing love in Jesus Christ. Christ has come. Christ is coming. Christ will come again. Look for the angels God has sent to you.

"Behold, I send my messenger/my angel to prepare the way before me," says the Lord. Who has served as God's messenger for you? Who has been a "refiner and purifier" of the precious depths of your heart? Who has helped to prepare you to receive the Lord? Who has helped you to hear the Advent message: Christ has come; Christ is coming; Christ will come again.

Think about this. You might be an angel to others. God may be using your gifts to touch the lives of persons who are in the midst of suffering or confusion. God may indeed be challenging you to be a Malachi (my angel) to others in need.

Where are these angels? They are all around us.

God is in the strong and loving discipline of Harold who teaches metal shop in an inner-city high school. Every Friday he invites troubled teens to spend the weekend on his farm, where they work, play, and pray together. When several young men were caught with guns and knives, Harold helped them to fashion a metal cross out of the weapons of violence. Those young men are now serving the Lord in their neighborhoods.

God is in the listening and accepting love of Carole, widowed twice in tragic circumstances. Carole has organized and leads a regional grief support team that ministers to and with hundreds of troubled persons. Her witness is contagious.

God is in the caring word and actions of Karen, whose father died when she was in grade school. For years she carried a small teddy bear, named Marvin, whose soft warmth provided a reminder of her heavenly Father's comfort in the midst of depression and confusion. As she grew in faith and courage Karen placed Marvin on a shelf in her pastor's office, asking the pastor to use Marvin's story to help other hurting children. Karen is now "a Marvin," an angel of comfort, as a therapist in a long-term care facility.

This day, open your eyes and see the messengers of the Lord surrounding you. This day, open your ears to hear the word of the Lord spoken by the Advent Angels in your midst. Look for the "motorboats and helicopters" God has sent to deliver you. This day, open your souls to perceive anew the presence and power of the crucified and risen Lord whom God has sent to redeem you. This day, resolve to be an Advent Angel to others in the name of the Lord.

Anticipation Proclamation

Advent 3   *Zephaniah 3:14-20*

During the spring of their senior year, seminary students begin the parish interview process in preparation for their first call as pastor. At one seminary, seniors are asked by a professor to respond to two specific questions.

The first question is: What expectations do lay persons have for their next pastor? Seniors are overwhelmed by their own responses, which include the following: visionary leader, dynamic preacher (interpreted as entertaining and brief), excellent administrator, caring counselor, frequent visitor, fabulous fund-raiser, great with youth and children and elderly, super evangelist (interpreted as recruit new members to help meet the budget), young but experienced, twenty-four-hour crisis availability, and willing to accept less than the recommended minimum compensation package. Seniors are stunned. After class, one told her professor, "They anticipate that I will be a Messiah." Great anticipation, but neither realistic or achievable.

The second question for these seminary students is: What do you expect from parishioners in your first congregation? Their answers are theologically articulate and conceptually sound. They focus on the theme of living out one's baptism as a member of the priesthood of believers. Now that's a theological mouthful! Students often expect their future parishioners to assume eagerly and willingly the actions of early Christians as evangelists, stewards, visitors of the sick and troubled, administrators, and teachers. Bible and prayer groups would abound. In their ideal congregation, parishioners would want their pastor to be a theologian-in-residence. They would hear the Word of God with joy and share the sacrament with zeal and excitement. They would be active in both member care and community outreach. They would bring an inclusive, open, and global perspective to ministry.

Wow! If parishioners are anticipating the Messiah, seminarians are anticipating doing ministry in the Messianic Kingdom of Glory.

Neither group seems to consider the reality of sin in this world. Neither group seems to attempt to discern the will and action of God in this process. Both groups anticipate that God would bring an immediate, permanent, and total change in the practical activities of their lives — according to their own wants and desires ... and right now.

This was definitely the situation of the people at the time of our text in Zephaniah. Great expectations. Great anticipations, yet there was no connection to God's will. They anticipated deliverance, right now. They anticipated the ideal Messianic Kingdom, right now. They anticipated that God as warrior-king would bring about a golden age according to their *own* wants and desires, right now.

Success in our time according to our own definition is still a major theme in our society today. However, God had something even better in store for the people in Zephaniah's time, and for you and me.

God's promised restoration was not just for the seventh century Jews. God's promise of joy is not just for twentieth century Americans. God's promise is for all persons in all times and in all places. "Sing, shout, rejoice with all your heart," exalts the prophet (verse 14). "Do not fear, let not your hands grow weak. The Lord, your God, is in your midst" (vv. 16-17).

This is the message Zephaniah's audience needed to hear. This is the Advent message we need to hear today. The Lord your God is in your midst right now. Sing, shout, rejoice with all your hearts.

Celebrate what God has already done. God does not forget God's people in the midst of sinful, troubled times. Remember God's mighty acts of deliverance in the flood and the exodus. Remember the birth of a baby in Bethlehem. The Lord your God is in your midst. Christ has come.

Nevertheless, we still live in a sinful world. Just getting through each day is a major challenge. It's hard to get by with only memories for support. Where is God in all this? What is God doing *now*? What can we celebrate *now*?

Celebrate what God is doing now in congregations across our nation. Christ is present as Dan organizes a youth group in serving meals in a homeless shelter and opens church doors to homeless families; Christ is present as Sarah coordinates a powerful ministry with AIDS victims and their families. Christ is present as Linda leads neighborhood residents in a prayerful march to bring the Gospel to victims of violence and drugs. Christ is present as Mary welcomes a lonely visitor during worship. The Lord is present as Reggie looks out over the ruins of a church building destroyed by arson and begins to mobilize a renewed Christ-centered inner-city ministry. "Do not let your hands grow weary," says Zephaniah. "The Lord your God is in your midst."

This almost sounds too easy, doesn't it? Sometimes quoting scripture or sharing examples of God's action in others' lives can seem like nonsense when we are in despair. When we need a miracle to find relief, we don't often want to hear simple stories of God's past actions, even if they *are* in the Bible. We want specific assurances of God's promises to us. We want precise promises for our future. And we want to celebrate them right *now*.

In times like this, it is difficult to learn from the experience of others. It is hard to make meaningful connections to the experience of God's people throughout history. It is a real uphill struggle to understand that God keeps promises of deliverance and strength for all God's children. It is no easy task even to remember our own past experiences of God's presence and guidance.

When our world becomes so narrow that we do not allow ourselves to learn from past experiences of God's loving relation-ships, we become like the woman in the following story. She had heard about a job opening in her firm that would mean a significant promotion for her. This would result in more money and increased status among her peers. It was the opportunity of a lifetime. She applied, but she did not get the position. Instead, another woman, who had been with the firm far less time than she, was promoted. When she complained to the Director of Human Resources, the Director responded, "I'm sorry, but you haven't had the 25 years of experience stated on your application. You've had only one year's experience repeated 25 times."

This unfortunate situation occurs far too often in our lives as Christians. The people in Zephaniah's time found it difficult to learn from their history as God's people. The woman in our story was unable to learn and to grow from her own experience. Perhaps the same is also true for us today.

The Lord our God is in our midst. Even now. The Lord our God was with our ancestors of old and is with us in the present. The biblical witness of that glorious fact is vibrant and alive. The witness of countless sisters and brothers in the faith today is exciting and energizing.

God keeps promises. We need to hear that good news again and again. God kept promises in the past. God keeps promises to us in the present. God will keep promises in the future. "The Lord, your God, is in your midst," Zephaniah rejoices, "the Lord will rejoice over you with gladness and will renew you in his love" (v. 17).

This promise is for us today. It is just as real today as it was for Zephaniah 2,600 years ago. The Lord speaks to us, saying, "I will save the lame and gather the outcast, and I will change their shame into praise" (v. 19).

So, then, do not let your hands grow weak. Learn from the collective experience of God's people. The Lord your God is in your midst and has promised to deliver you. That's a *fact*. That's *reason* to rejoice.

Here is Zephaniah's "anticipation proclamation." Here is the good news of Advent. Christ has come. Christ is coming. Christ will come again.

Tiny Town: Promised Power

Advent 4   *Micah 5:2-5a*

Country and western music tells stories of broken dreams and sad times. The mournful lyrics are often cries of hopelessness, helplessness, and insignificance in the overall scheme of things. Perhaps you are familiar with titles like these: "Every Time I Make My Mark, Somebody Paints The Wall"; "Here's A Quarter, Call Someone Who Cares"; "I'm Standing In The Middle Of The River And Dying Of Thirst"; "Why Don't Your Dog Bite Nobody But Me?"; "There's A Light At The End Of The Tunnel; Lord, I Hope It Ain't No Train."

God tells us in today's text that there is indeed a light at the end of the dark and dreary tunnel, and that light shines from the tiny, little insignificant town of Bethlehem Ephrathah. There is a light at the end of the tunnel and it is truly the Light of the World, Jesus the Christ. Here again is the Advent theme: The Light has come; the Light is coming; the Light will come again.

Sometimes, however, it is hard to accept that light as a very real part of our lives, especially when things go wrong ... when we discover over and over again that life isn't always fair ... when those country and western songs seem to be describing our own lives.

Things were certainly going wrong in Judah during Micah's era of the late eighth century B.C. The Assyrian army had conquered Northern Israel. Although Judah was spared at the time, political turmoil soon left Judah as a wrecked vassal state with Assyrian forces at its borders. Micah saw corruption among political, business, and religious leaders. He saw no hope in military efforts. Micah saw a coming destruction. However, he also saw that a remnant would be gathered by the Lord (2:12f; 5:7f). Micah saw that light at the end of the tunnel all right — and the tunnel's end was not in the powerful fortress of Jerusalem. It was not under the tower of the citadel of David. At tunnel's end the light would shine from that tiny, insignificant little town, Bethlehem, of the tiny, most insignificant clan of Ephrathah — the birthplace of Jesus the Christ.

"But you, O Bethlehem Ephrathah, who are little to be among the clans of Judah," states Micah, "from you shall come forth for me one who is to be ruler in Israel, whose origin is from of old, from ancient days."

What about you, O sister and brother in Christ? Do you ever perceive yourselves as weak, helpless, and surrounded by pressures and powers beyond your control? Do you ever feel like a tiny, insignificant speck on the landscape of life around you? Do you ever feel as if you are, in the words of ELCA Bishop H. George Anderson, "Nothing more than an itch on the Body of Christ"? I know that I do.

We need a word from God. Where is God in all this? Today, that word comes from Micah. Listen again to his words, and this time substitute your name or the name of your community or congregation in the blank spaces. "And you O ___, ___ who are little among the clans of ___, from you shall come forth for me one who is to be ruler in ___, whose origin is from of old, from ancient days."

Here is The Word from God for you and me from ancient days. Christ has come! Christ is coming! Christ will come again! Christ came to us at baptism. Christ is with us now. Christ will come again. Alleluia!

You see, from insignificance comes promised power in the Lord. Micah declares that the promised Shepherd King from tiny little Bethlehem Ephrathah "shall stand and feed his flock in the strength of the Lord" (v. 4). Now, nourishment and strength do not always refer to promises of physical well-being, earthly power, and personal status. They come from the Lord.

Did you ever think that perhaps God's strength for you and for the Church might originate more in the love of Christ and less in the stories of Horatio Alger? During the nineteenth century, Alger became famous for writing over 100 novels featuring rags-to-riches stories that became the epitome of the American dream. The principle character invariably started life in poverty, experiencing a series of rejections and failures. Then, through a refusal to give up and a renewed dedication to succeed, the hero would basically pull himself out of poverty by his own bootstraps. Success and power were the certain result. Happy endings became the trademark of an Alger novel.

Alger's own life, however, did not have a happy ending. Disillusioned with writing, he tried many jobs with little success and less fulfillment. Eventually he suffered an emotional breakdown. Horatio Alger, whose name became synonymous with achievement of wealth and happiness, died penniless and miserable.

Success is not a "rags-to-riches" story of self-help and achievement. Happiness is not accomplished through our own efforts to realize our "full potential." True meaning and purpose in life, authentic success, is only found in the free gift of God in Jesus Christ.

True nourishment and strength are not obtained through what money can buy or personal status can achieve. Nourishment is given to you, *for* you in the bread and wine at the Lord's table. This meal nourishes the soul, forgives the sinful heart, and renews the relationship that sustains in the midst of life's turmoil. Strength is given in the power of the cross that leads us to face with courage the forces of evil that surround us.

Throughout history, every time God's people found success, something bad seemed to happen. The Assyrians conquered northern Israel. The Babylonians destroyed Jerusalem and took its leading citizens into exile. The Saleucian Greeks sacked the Jerusalem Temple and sacrificed pigs in its courtyard. The Romans carried out a terrible persecution of Christians. The powerful church of the Middle Ages crumbled from inner corruption. The Holy Catholic Church became a church fragmented by parochial and nationalistic concerns.

You see, our identity as the children of God is not based on success and stability according to the world's standards. Success in the eyes of the world is definitely short-lived. Something always happens that turns our lives into the laments of country and western music. Something always happens to bring us to our knees; to bring us to the true source of our identity, Jesus Christ. Promised power comes from within an awareness of the security given in the blood of Christ and not by the sweat of our own brows or by the efforts of anyone else. The Christ of Bethlehem Ephrathah brings significance to our lives. The Christ of Bethlehem Ephrathah makes us special people, God's people.

A friend's daughter spells her name Katy. On her first day of kindergarten, her teacher asked her to spell her name. "K-A-T-Y," she replied. "That's interesting," responded the teacher. "Most little girls I know with that name spell it K-A-T-I-E. I wonder why yours is different."

"I don't know," said Katy. "That's just the way Jesus wants it. I guess I'm just special."

Well, Katy might not always enjoy the success that either she or her parents desire. Yet she will always know that she is special because that is the way Jesus wants it. And so will we. That's what God has promised. With Katy, we know that this promise *is* sure and certain, and forever. Micah proclaims, "And they shall live secure, for now he shall be great to the ends of the earth; and he shall be the one of peace" (vv. 4-5).

The identity of God's children is always shaped at the foot of the cross and not in a story by Horatio Alger. In the Christ of Bethlehem Ephrathah comes promised power.

Tiny town, promised power, for Bethlehem Ephrathah, for our congregations, and for you and me. God's promises *do not fail*. God's peace nourishes and strengthens. The powerful Light of Christ shines through the darkened tunnels of our lives.

Unexpected Joy; Undeserved Gift

Christmas Eve/Day *Isaiah 9:2-7*

Choosing a baby's name is tough! Most of us have been involved in that process at some time in our lives and we know this from personal experience. We have consulted numerous books and reviewed family histories in our search for just the right name. A name connects memory and hope, promise and power, past and future. Choosing a name is a major step in shaping a child's identity. Choosing a name is the beginning of charting a child's future. Choosing a name is serious business.

> ... *and he is named Wonderful Counselor, Mighty God, Everlasting Father, Prince of Peace.* (v. 6)

Here Isaiah lists ceremonial names given to the king at his coronation. These names reaffirmed the Lord's covenant with David 200 years ago. These names expressed desire that the people's hopes for renewal of spirit and restoration of power would occur. These names express a yearning for a new identity, a new vision that will emerge during the reign of a wise and powerful king. These names are full of power and promise. These names connect memories of the past and hopes for the future.

This king would demonstrate fatherly love and care. This king would restore harmony and peace in a land tottering on the brink of destruction by the powerful Assyrian army on its borders and by moral and religious corruption among its leaders. The people of Judah were living in a land of deep darkness all right (v. 2). Their memories of past power and glory under David were but a dimly glowing ember. The people of Judah were ready for a new and brilliant light. They were ready for some unexpected joy.

This story is told about the famous American inventor Thomas Edison. When the Western Union Telegraph Company offered to purchase Edison's newly invented ticker, he had no idea how much to ask for it. He puzzled over this for several days, but was unable to arrive at a price. Finally, Edison's wife grew tired of his brooding and suggested that he ask $20,000. Reluctantly, he agreed, but he believed that this figure was far too high. No invention of his was worth that much.

When Western Union officials asked his price, Edison stood speechless. He had great difficulty in naming an amount that was so ridiculously high. After several uncomfortable minutes of silence, a Western Union representative blurted out, "How about $100,000?"

Unexpected joy! And, in Edison's view, an undeserved gift!

This was the nature of God's promise to the beleaguered people of Judah in Isaiah's time. They were desperately ready for unexpected joy. They were hoping for an undeserved gift. They were eager for a new birth. They were ready to celebrate.

And we are, also! A day doesn't pass when we don't hear stories of terrorism and violence, church burnings and drive-by shootings, theft and corruption, pain and sadness. Each Christmas season we strive desperately for the perfect party, the perfect family gathering, the perfect gift to drive away the dark times. And we come away empty. We discover again, sadly, that these efforts are meaningless and a striving after the wind (Ecclesiastes 2:11).

Our own efforts to bring any light into our darkness are just as futile as trying to nail a raindrop to a windowpane. We need God to do something! We are more than eager for some unexpected joy. We need something new; something to celebrate; something from God. We need something joyful.

Friends, that joy is here today. The King is in our midst today. The baby is born today. "For to us a child is born (today), to us a son is given (today) ... and his name is called Wonderful Counselor, Mighty God, Everlasting Father, Prince of Peace."

These titles for a new king in Judah have become new names for the King of all nations and for all times, Jesus the Christ. Georg Friedrich Handel placed these names at the center of his "For Unto Us A Child Is Born" in Part I of the *Messiah*. The booming strains of this music fill our souls with joy:

> *For to us a child is born,*
> *Unto us a son is given ...*
> *And his name shall be called*
> *Wonderful Counselor, Mighty God,*
> *Everlasting Father, Prince of Peace.*

The names of our new king have been chosen. Our new identity has been forged. The promises of the past are coming alive in the present. Our hope for the future is assured. Jesus Christ is born today. The light of joy shines brightly in our darkened world. Hallelujah!

Becky and Joe were told by doctors that Becky would be unable to bear children. Their sorrow was enormous. Their dreams of family were shattered. Then, after several years — an unexpected gift. Becky was pregnant. Days, weeks, then months passed ever so slowly, filled with hope, and tinged with fear. Whatever might happen was in God's hands. And early one morning, amidst tears and shouts and high fives, Becky and Joe and a multitude of the heavenly host of family, friends, and parishioners greeted a six-pound five-ounce gift from God, Stephen John. "For to us a child is born, to us a son is given," declares Isaiah. Now, this birth indeed was good news, glorious news for Becky and Joe. This unexpected gift was celebrated for months by friends and family and church members. For them this birth also pointed to something more. The birth of Stephen (and later, his brother Charles!) pointed to the birth of all births.

Of course, not all are able to experience such a miraculous pregnancy and birth in their own families. Carolyn and Fred were informed by their physician that, due to Carolyn's health, pregnancy was out of the question, so they chose to adopt children who were physically and developmentally challenged. They tell everyone who will listen that each child is a gift of love — a gift from God. For Carolyn and Fred, each new arrival into their family is truly the arrival of the Christ Child.

Betty is a retired high school teacher and a widow. She spends several days each week volunteering in a facility that provides care for children with AIDS. She says that whenever she looks into the eyes of one of these children, she knows that she is gazing upon the face of the Baby Jesus.

Isaiah proclaims, "For a child has been born for us, a son is given to us" (v. 6). Who is that child for you? Where do you see the Christ Child? When do you gaze upon the face of the Baby Jesus?

Look around you and see the joy we celebrate today. Look around you today and experience the renewed promise of hope and strength that God has placed inside the manger of our hearts. Listen again to the words of the angel to the shepherds on that glorious night of nights: "Do not be afraid. I bring you good news of great joy which will come to all people; for to you is born this day in the city of David, a Savior who is Christ the Lord" (Luke 2:10-11).

That angel speaks to us, today. To us, indeed, a child is born! To us, indeed, a son is given. Hallelujah! To us is born, in times of deep darkness, a child, who is Christ the Lord. To us, who live in bondage to sin, an undeserved gift is given. In the giving of this gift, God gives us a new identity — loved, forgiven, chosen child. In the giving of this gift, God has placed our source of hope not in the coronation of a powerful military and political leader, but in a baby — born in a stable. In the giving of this gift, God has placed our strength not at the throne of a king, but at the foot of the cross. For to us a child is born, to us a son is given; an undeserved gift, an unexpected joy. Thank God!

Gifts: Rejected And Exchanged, Accepted And Shared

Christmas 1   *1 Samuel 2:18-20, 26*

So, what have you been doing since Christmas Day? If you are like most people in the community, you have been spending countless hours in shopping malls, looking for bargains and exchanging gifts. Retailers tell us that their busiest times are the days immediately after Thanksgiving and the days directly following Christmas. After Thanksgiving we begin gift buying in earnest. After Christmas, we begin the exchanging and bargain hunting frenzy.

What happened with the gifts you chose to give? How were they received? What did that feel like for you? What happened to the gifts you received? How did you react? What did that feel like?

The Christmas season is all about giving and receiving gifts. It's easy to allow ourselves to become so caught up in the choosing and wrapping, the unwrapping and exchanging that we miss one crucial fact. Each gift represents the identity of the giver and its connection to the identity of the receiver. Each gift is an "integration of identities," an offering of oneself to another, a receiving of oneself by another. Each gift can represent a relationship between giver and receiver. Each gift can represent a relationship given, a relationship accepted, and a relationship shared.

Where is God in all this?

The story of Samuel's birth and dedication to the Lord is a fine example of this relationship (1 Samuel 1 and 2). Remember that

Samuel's mother, Hannah, had been barren for many years. In spite of being the object of ridicule and scorn (1:6) and suffering from deep sadness (1:16), Hannah remained in faithful relationship to the Lord. Hoping against all hope, she continued in prayer to God.

And the gift was given. A son was born. A relationship was offered, accepted, and shared. Hannah dedicated the young child to the Lord. After Samuel was weaned, Hannah and her husband, Elkanah, presented him to Eli, the priest of the Lord, at Shiloh. Samuel, bearing the "name of God," began his training as a priest of God. A relationship was given by the Lord to Hannah. A relationship was shared by Hannah with the Lord.

Here is where our text begins.

Each year Hannah used to make a linen robe (ephod) for Samuel and bring it along with them when she and her husband made their yearly sacrifice to the Lord at Shiloh. A gift given; a gift shared. As they approached, Hannah and Elkanah saw their young son wearing the ceremonial priestly linen apron, ministering before the Lord (2:18-19). What joy must have filled their hearts! A relationship was given; a relationship was accepted; a relationship was shared with the Lord.

Doesn't this put our own Christmas gift giving and receiving in a different perspective? The size and color may not matter so much anymore. The price wars and labels may take on less meaning. The number of "batteries-not-included" and "some-assembly-required" notations may not be so intimidating. Gifts are offerings of relationships, to be rejected and exchanged, or accepted and shared. Of course, practical issues must also be considered. Exchanges do happen. Nevertheless, the gift of relationship remains central. The offering of an even deeper relationship is beneath the ribbons and wrappings.

So, what have you been doing since Christmas Day? How have you encountered the offering of relationship? Has your response been one of rejecting or accepting? Refusing or sharing?

Continuing with our text, we see that the accepted relationship continues to grow. More gifts are given. More gifts are shared. Deeper relationships are experienced. During their annual visit to Shiloh, Eli, the priest, would bless Elkanah and his wife. He would say to Elkanah, "May the Lord give you children by this woman for the petition she asked of the Lord" (v. 20). Then the proud parents would return to their home.

The section missing from our text (vv. 21-25) provides more insight into the contrasting manner in which gifts are received and shared. On the one hand, during the ensuing years, Hannah and Elkanah did indeed receive more gifts. "And the Lord visited Hannah, and she conceived and bore three sons and two daughters. And the boy Samuel [also] grew in the presence of the Lord" (v. 21). The text later states, again, that "the boy Samuel continued to grow both in stature and in favor with the Lord and with all persons" (v. 26).

On the other hand, the following three verses (vv. 22-25) describe how Eli's sons received the gift of relationship with the Lord. These children of the priest, who were raised in a holy place, in the midst of holy things, were incorrigible. Instead of accepting and sharing their gift, these young men had become so corrupt and immoral that no one, not even their father, could intercede for them. Their fate was sealed. They had brought it upon themselves. A gift given. A gift rejected. A relationship offered. A relationship refused.

So, what have you been doing since Christmas Day? How did you accept the greatest gift ever given, the baby Jesus? How are you sharing that gift? What's happening with the other Christmas relationships that were offered around the Christmas tree at your house?

Three-year-old Tyler was just learning the Lord's Prayer. At bedtime on Christmas Eve, Tyler knelt at his bedside, all by himself, and began to pray. Parents and grandparents huddled just outside the door, listening proudly for the Lord's Prayer. Well, they heard it all right, through the first four petitions. Then Tyler began on his own "unauthorized translation." Just after "give us this day our daily bread," Tyler prayed, "And forgive us our *Christmases* as we forgive those who *Christmas* against us." Oops!

Of course, little Tyler probably confused the unknown and distant "trespass" with the known and familiar "Christmas." Or did he? Could Tyler's "unauthorized translation" have been a nudge from the Holy Spirit? What was Christmas really like as seen through Tyler's three-year-old eyes? What was your Christmas really like?

Jennifer's father was accustomed to bringing home a briefcase full of work from the office. After a quick supper he would retreat to the den and immerse himself in one project or other, shutting off the world around him. One evening, four-year-old Jennifer dared to enter her father's inner sanctum. "Daddy," she said with that charming and irresistible voice, "will you read to me?"

Jennifer's father looked at the mass of paperwork spread across his desk. He felt the pressure of an impending deadline at work. Then he looked again into the deep blue eyes of his daughter. "Hop up here, Jennifer," he said. "Let's see what *The Cat In The Hat* is up to tonight."

A gift given. A relationship offered. A relationship accepted. What relationships have been offered to you this Christmas season? What relationships have you accepted?

There is a Middle Eastern legend that tells the story of a desert wanderer who happened upon a spring of clear, sweet water. It was so refreshing that he decided to bring his king a sample. Filling his leather canteen, the traveler began a lengthy journey in the hot sun to the palace.

Unknown to the traveler, when he finally reached his destination, the water had become stale within its leather container. However, the king graciously accepted the gift of his faithful subject. He drank deeply, with an expression of gratitude and fulfillment. The traveler departed with joy in his heart.

After he had gone, other members of the king's court tasted the stale water and asked why the king had pretended to enjoy it. "It was not the water I tasted," replied the king. "I tasted the spirit in which it was given."

Underneath the traveler's gift was an offering of relationship to be refused and rejected, or accepted and shared. This Christmas season many gifts have been given. Many relationships have been offered. Underneath the wrappings and ribbons are relationship opportunities that can be shared and multiplied in the name of Christ.

A wondrous gift is indeed given, to you and to all people. A child is born to you and all people. Let this gift, like the boy, Samuel, grow both in stature and in favor with all people. Let this marvelous gift of loving relationship bloom and grow in your hearts so that others, too, might see the gift above all gifts, and the king above all kings, Jesus Christ our Lord.

An Awesome Homecoming

Christmas 2 *Jeremiah 31:7-14*

Many people enjoy jogging early in the morning, when the mist still clings to the trees and tall grass that line the roadside. Cardinals and Carolina wrens have just begun singing their wake-up calls to the sun. A family of deer gathers at the edge of the woods lining the pasture. God is in heaven and all is right with the world.

Not today. Two hundred yards ahead, on the only road leading home, looms a huge, dark, teeming mass of something alive and menacing, stretching from one side of the road to the other. In the dim light of pre-dawn it looks like a creature from one of those late night fright movies on television. Going around it is impossible. There is swamp land on each side. Who knows what terrible, slimy creatures lie in wait just beneath those scummy waters? Turning back means another hour and crossing an interstate highway. Home is just ahead. And so is that treacherous blob.

As our jogger approaches, this mountain of dread becomes a glob of about fifty turkey vultures; huge, greedy, grasping birds with dark feathers and naked heads that feed on carrion. What if they think he is road kill? He picks up some gravel and runs faster, arms flailing wildly and screaming at the top of his voice. Ever so slowly the mound begins to shrink as one by one the vultures rise with a whoosh of wings and lurk on the low-lying branch of an oak tree. Their long, thin necks and sharp beaks point directly at his head as he runs below.

It's over. Home is a few minutes down the road. Thank God! Remember that Tony Orlando and Dawn song about a man returning home from prison, "Tie A Yellow Ribbon Around The Old Oak Tree"? That was the way our jogger felt. The prisoner is free. Home is on the horizon. Get out the yellow ribbons, Ma, Bubba is comin' home!

Today's text in Jeremiah is also a joyful song of deliverance. It is a song of homecoming for a shattered and scattered Israel. A century before, powerful Assyrian armies had conquered northern Israel and dispersed its inhabitants throughout the far corners of Assyria's vast empire. There was no earthly hope of restoration and return. Most had become absorbed by the political structures and religious practices of the cultures in which they had relocated. Connections to their faithful heritage were but a dim memory, fading rapidly for all but a few. Visions of a road home were blinded by a dark, teeming mass of menacing troops, bandits, and wild animals waiting to pounce upon anyone who dared to test their power. Where is God in all this? What will God say about this? What will God do about this?

"For thus says the Lord," Jeremiah proclaims. Before going farther, we need to understand that when Jeremiah uses this phrase, he intends for all to know that the following is to be understood as the word of the Lord (*Dabar Adonai* in Hebrew) and not Jeremiah's. Jeremiah begins prophecies of doom and gloom with this phrase (23:16; 24:8, 15). Here in this passage Jeremiah can speak God's word with excitement. Note the verbs are full of joy. The Lord will describe both what the Lord has done and will do, in loving faithfulness. "Sing aloud with great joy; proclaim, give praise." Why? The Lord "has saved, ransomed and redeemed" the scattered and shattered remnant (vv. 7, 11). The Lord "will gather" them from the farthest parts of the earth (v. 8) and "will keep them as a shepherd keeps his flock" (v. 10). The Lord "will turn their mourning into joy. The Lord will comfort them and give them gladness for sorrow." Now that's a joyful homecoming! That's worth singing about! Get out the yellow ribbons. God's people are free to come home again.

However, experience tells us that joyful homecomings also bring hard work, difficult challenges, and discouraging tasks. A few years ago the residents of the South Carolina coast from Charleston to Myrtle Beach were forced to evacuate their homes in preparation for the violent onslaught of Hurricane Hugo. Six-lane interstate highways moved traffic only one way – away from the coast. Hugo was a huge storm that brought winds in excess of 140 miles per hour and a tidal surge of nineteen feet. The hurricane destroyed nearly everything in its path. When the governor declared it was finally safe to return, people arrived in shock. Homes and places of business had been turned to rubble. National Guard troops patrolled the streets to prevent looting and to distribute food and water. Temporary shelters were constructed. And "temporary" stretched from days into weeks and even months.

Homecoming isn't always easy. What has it been like for you now that the holiday season has drawn to a close? For some, homes filled to overflowing with visiting friends and relatives are now empty. For others, homes standing empty during the holidays are now reoccupied by families getting ready to resume work and school activities. And for some, homes that were lonely during Christmas and New Year's Day still remain lonely today.

Routines begin again. Problems put on hold for a few weeks begin to surface anew. Visions of sugarplum fairies bringing continuing joy and everlasting peace are shattered and scattered, at least until next year, just like the Christmas decorations. Christmas trees, or those "previously live" ones, are carted out for curbside pick up. Christmas promises and expectations are not what we had hoped for ... again. Or are they?

The true Christmas promise was born in the insignificant little town of Bethlehem, not in the powerful empire capital of Rome, or even in the principal city of Palestine, Jerusalem. The true Christmas promise was not a commitment to overthrow the Roman army or the misguided religious and political leaders of Jerusalem. The true Christmas promise was not an immediate end to all evil and suffering.

Instead, the Christmas promise was and is Jesus the Christ, son of the living God. It was and is a promise of love and faithfulness that leads to the cross. It was and is a promise that leads to forgiveness and hope, overcoming our bondage to sin and suffering, and uniting us in a community bound by baptism, not by ties of family name, race, gender, or geography. Perhaps our Christmas expectations need a different focus. Perhaps there is a deeper quality to homecoming.

Remember those Christmas trees ready for the trash? Many Christians strip the limbs and fashion a cross from the remaining trunk. The cross is prominently displayed during the Lenten season, in preparation for the triumph of Easter.

The true Christmas homecoming is a journey to the cross and a participation in a loving and faithful community. It is a journey that gathers people from the farthest parts of the earth, the blind and the lame, the pregnant and the barren, the remembered and the forgotten. It is a journey of promise, a journey of joy. And you are invited, by the Lord, to join up (v. 8)!

It's a grand and glorious journey, a magnificent homecoming. "Young women shall dance for you and young men and old shall make merry," sings Jeremiah. The Lord will "turn grieving into joy, and give gladness for sorrow" (v. 13).

Get out the yellow ribbons! That dark blot in the road has been conquered by the cross. Jesus has invited you on a marvelous, awesome journey home.

Reach For
The Light

Epiphany　　　　　　　　　　　　　　　　*Isaiah 60:1-6*

What's the first thing you do when you awaken from a scary dream? Exactly! Most of us reach for the light. Our rational minds tell us that it was nothing but a dream. It wasn't real. However, our bodies aren't convinced. We want to put our pillows over our heads and bury ourselves beneath all the blankets. But, it won't work. Our hearts are pumping and thumping. Arteries are stretched to the limit by blood racing to our feet and hands. Lungs strain to take in as much oxygen as possible. Adrenal glands work arduously to prepare us to flee or to fight unknown demons of the night. Reach for the light, now, before it's too late!

Since the beginning of time humans have sought the light around campfires, candles and torches at the approach of darkness. Light promises hope and warmth, safety and security. Deep within the human heart the onset of darkness stirs up unknown fears of forces of evil beyond our control. Darkness and light call forth contrasts of despair and joy; evil and good; weakness and strength; sin and salvation; shame and glory. Reach for the light, tonight, before it's too late!

The festival of the Epiphany of Our Lord is a celebration that has reminded Christians since the second century that the light has already reached us. The light has already come in Jesus Christ. His light has vanquished the dark nightmares in our souls.

"Arise, shine;" declares Isaiah, "for your light has come, and the glory of the Lord has risen upon you" (v. 1). Nightmares exist. Evil lurks around darkened corners of our lives, "but the Lord will arise upon you and his glory will appear over you" (v. 2).

Did you catch the language of both Christmas and Easter here? The Light has come. The Glory of the Lord has risen. It is no coincidence that early Christians selected this text to be read on Epiphany Day, the day on which the appearance of the Light of Christ is celebrated. The Light, born in Bethlehem, rises and shines brilliantly from the empty tomb outside Jerusalem. Epiphany, the Day of Light, connects birth, passion, and resurrection in the Church year. The Light has reached us. The Light shines in our lives tonight.

In many congregations throughout the world the celebration of this festival begins with a darkened sanctuary. Worshipers are given candles as they enter. The worship leader processes slowly towards the chancel, following an acolyte carrying one large lighted candle, which is placed in its stand in front of the congregation.

In dialogue the leader and worshipers proclaim, "Jesus Christ is the Light of the World, the Light which no darkness can overcome. Stay with us, Lord, for it is evening and the day is almost over. Let your light scatter the darkness and illumine your Church." Candles of those gathered are lighted from the larger flame. "Arise, shine; for your Light has come, and the Glory of the Lord has risen upon you" (v. 1).

In John 1:14, we hear this presented in another way: "And the Word became Flesh and dwelt among us, full of grace and truth; we have beheld His glory, glory as of the only Son from the Father." In biblical language, the word for "dwell" can be literally translated as "build a tabernacle" or "pitch a tent." Jesus, the very Word of God, the true Light, pitched a tent in our midst and chose to live among us. The glory of the risen Christ remains with us. Arise, shine, for your Light has come!

What does this mean for us?

In today's lesson Isaiah pictures Jerusalem (Zion) as a woman prostrate on the ground at the beginning of the New Year covenant renewal celebration. Zion is bidden to rise and see what the Lord is doing and will do in her midst. Perhaps this is the Lord's word for us as well. Arise, wake up from the nightmares in the world around us. The demons in our own darkness will not prevail. With the Magi from the East, look for the brilliant star. "Lift up your eyes and see" (v. 4). Let the true Light overcome our midnight anxiety. But, we have to look up for the Light. We can't discover the Light by hiding beneath the covers of self-protection and fear. The Magi looked up, saw the light, and followed it to a manger, the birthplace of a king. It wasn't an easy journey. They faced all the hazards of a long journey across the wilderness. They faced the evil of treacherous King Herod. Yet they persisted, in faith, proceeding onward, following wherever the light might lead them.

Following a long and bitter congregational conflict, a pastor was asked what kept her going until reconciliation and renewal finally resulted. She replied, "The Five *P*'s of ministry: Prayer, Persistence, Prayer, Play, and Prayer." Notice that prayer was at the beginning, middle, and end of her list. Prayer connects us to the true Light. Prayer keeps the vision of the true Light in view as darkness threatens to overcome it. Prayer enables us to place one foot in front of the other in the long and difficult journey through unknown darkness. Reach for the true Light in prayer. Lift up your eyes to see the guiding light of Christ along your life journey.

Pay careful attention to what our text says happens when we journey in this light. Using vivid imagery here, Isaiah states that nations surrounding Jerusalem will see what the Lord has done and come to pay tribute and join in the celebration. "And nations will come to your light ...They all gather and come to you" (vv.3-4). Listen again to this important promise: "... nations will *come to your light*. They will gather and *come to you*."

You see, the Light shining in our midst is contagious. The Light that guides our journey gathers others along the way. Reach for the Light. Celebrate the Light. Share the Light with others. "Then," declares Isaiah, "you shall see and be radiant, your heart shall thrill and rejoice" (v. 5).

There appear to be several significant factors present in healthy, vital, faithful congregations. Although there are many variables, one principal feature has emerged. This is the eagerness of members to share faith stories, their journey in the Light with one another and in their neighborhoods. Members eagerly share "Where Is God In All This?" stories for themselves and their congregations. They share them as part of committee and choir devotions, in temple talks during worship, in Sunday School classes, and in parish retreats. No, they are not "fanatics." They are just like you and me, struggling against the darkness that threatens to overcome us all. More than today's typical "sideline" Christian, these folks have let God become the subject of more verbs in their vocabularies. They have taken seriously Isaiah's call to arise, and shine, for they know that their Light, our Light, has indeed come.

How did they develop this amazing power of witness? In each congregation opportunities were provided for persons to share, at whatever level they felt comfortable. And share they did. They described their own experiences of darkness and their own perceptions of seeing the light of Christ shine through. There was no gimmickry here. There were no terrific techniques for this. They simply took advantage of every possible opportunity. The Light did the rest.

The Light beckons; we do not. The Light gathers in; we do not. You and I are not contagious; but the Light is. Share the Light. Reflect it to others who walk in darkness. Reflect it to those who wake in chaos.

As Isaiah reminds us again, "Arise, shine; for your Light has come, and the glory of the Lord has risen upon you" (v. 1). Reach for the Light. Christ, the Light of the world, shines now in and for you.

Named And Claimed

Baptism Of The Lord   **Isaiah 43:1-7**

Have you ever watched children choosing up sides for a game? It seems as if certain children always get chosen first: the taller, stronger, more athletic, more intelligent, more popular. As more names are called and teams are formed, inevitably there is a small huddle of children standing off to the side trying to pretend that it doesn't matter. But it does. It matters and it hurts. These children can't help but overhear the scornful laughter and humiliating names aimed in their direction.

Remember that old adage, "Sticks and stones may break my bones, but names will never hurt me"? Well, that's wrong. Many of us carry deep scars in our hearts well into adulthood from just such experiences of taunting and rejection. Many of us still allow the shame of being among the last chosen to shape our present identities and behaviors. "Why bother trying? I can't do that anyway"; or, "If I do that, everyone will laugh"; or, "Nobody likes me, so why should I care about them?" or, "I'm not going to get close to anybody; I will just be rejected anyway." We have all heard phrases like this echoing deep within our psyches.

You know, it's just this kind of self-protection that often keeps us on the fringes of life, sadly watching others risking and enjoying. It's kind of like being a backseat driver in the tunnel of love. Of course, being last chosen for a game of kickball in the third grade is not at the core of every negative feeling we have about ourselves.

That's ridiculous. Nevertheless, we all have had similar experiences. Each of us can identify with those feelings of helplessness and powerlessness; feelings of having little control of our lives or of being at the mercy of the whims and choices of other people.

Corporate downsizing has resulted in many skilled workers losing employment. Changes in economic policies have eliminated many family farming operations. The increased mobility in our society has separated supportive extended families by hundreds, even thousands of miles. It's scary out there now. Too many names seem to be the first rejected, last selected. Where is hope? Where is a promise we can really count on? Where is a word from the Lord?

"But now, thus says the Lord," states Isaiah, "the one who created you, O Jacob, the one who formed you, O Israel" (v. 1a). Here the Lord speaks to the lost and rejected. "Remember the one who created you, the one who has chosen you," says the Lord. This section of the book of Isaiah was addressed to the Jews living in exile in Babylonia as a result of the conquest of Judah by King Nebuchadnezzar in the sixth century B.C. The Temple in Jerusalem was destroyed. City walls were left in ruins. Families were separated. The entire nation was in chaos. All the symbols of identity as a people and nation were demolished. They were exiles and losers, a forgotten people. The once proud name of Zion became a symbol of shame and degradation. Sound familiar? The word of the Lord came to them and the Lord comes to us today, through this passage in Isaiah.

The Lord created and formed Israel and Judah. They would not be forgotten. They have been chosen first, elected and selected to bear God's creating and redeeming word to all nations. Through Jesus Christ, the Lord has created and formed you and me. We are not forgotten. We, too, have been elected and selected to bear God's creative and redeeming word to all the world. What a text for baptism this is! What a text to remind us that God has chosen us! The word of the Lord continues: "Fear not, for I have redeemed you" (v. 1b). No more bondage to the forces that separate and humiliate. No more bondage to the power of sin. Here is deliverance.

"I have called you by name, you are mine," says the Lord (v. 1b). Here is precisely what happens at baptism. Here the Lord names us "chosen child of God." Here God claims us as members of an elite varsity team. No more embarrassed huddling on the sidelines. God has made us members of a vast community that has no boundaries of time or place. We are baptized. We are named and claimed by Christ himself, whose baptism we celebrate today.

Isaiah continues, addressing the Jewish exiles and using images of the Exodus from Egypt. Because God has chosen them, they will not live in exile forever. Because God has chosen them, they will not lose their identity as God's named and claimed people. Their return to Zion will be made smooth. Their protection is assured.

The word of the Lord promises them, "When you pass through the waters I will be with you; and through the rivers, they shall not overwhelm you; when you walk through fire, you shall not be burned, and the flame shall not consume you" (v. 2). This is also the word of the Lord to us today. We are baptized! The Lord has named and claimed us as adopted children of God. Certainly there are now, and will be in our future, times when we perceive ourselves to be drowning in the troubles of life. Certainly there are now, and will be in our future, times when it seems as if we are either burning out or dropping out from the pressures of daily existence. But God is with us. God has chosen us. God did not abandon the exiles. God will not abandon us. We are baptized!

There certainly will be times when it seems as if the blazing fires of family problems or work or school conflict are about to consume us. It would be easy to surrender. But God is with us. We are baptized! The Lord has called us by name. The Lord has chosen us. We belong to the Lord.

Like the exiles in Babylonia, we cannot save ourselves. But God has. God does. God will. "For I am the Lord your God, the Holy One of Israel, your savior," says the Lord (v. 3). Why does God promise this to a people that consistently rejected covenants and abandoned commitments? Why does God promise this to us? It does not make sense. It just isn't rational. The only answer God gives is one from the heart, not from the head. "Because you are precious in my eyes, and honored, and I love you" (v. 4). We are baptized into this amazing, overwhelming, irrational love made visible in the baptism and presence of Jesus Christ, the beloved Son in our midst. We are named and claimed by the steadfast love of the Lord. There is a marvelous story that illustrates this love.

Four-year-old Virginia and her family were enjoying the first visit by their new pastor. Gathered around the living room were Mother, Father, Virginia, Grandmother and the pastor. Soon it was Virginia's bedtime. After a bath, Virginia invited everyone to come up and hear her bedside prayers. Grandmother, whose arthritis was bothering her, chose not to go upstairs with the others and remained seated on the sofa. Just as Virginia knelt down, a flash of lightning followed by a crash of thunder filled the room. "I want to go downstairs with Grandmother," cried Virginia. "I'm scared."

The adults in the room tried to reassure her. "Jesus is right here with you," said Mother. "He's even in your closet and under your bed," added Father. The new pastor said, "Yes, remember, Virginia, Jesus is right here in your bedroom." Suddenly another blinding flash of lightning and deafening blast of thunder rattled the windows. Virginia, pointing a finger directly at the pastor, said through clenched teeth, "You stay up here in my bedroom with Jesus. I'm going downstairs to my grandmother's lap!" And off she ran.

You see, baptism is something like Grandmother's lap. In the midst of the rejections and raging storms of life, baptism reminds us where the love is. Named and claimed as God's child forever, we know that we have been chosen. No matter what. Hear again the promise of the Lord: "I have called you by name and you are mine ... you are precious in my eyes, and honored, and I love you" (vv. 1, 4). And that's the truth.

New Name, New Status

Epiphany 2   *Isaiah 62:1-5*

Have you ever listened to young children at play and noticed that they often give themselves new names? The names may be those of a superhero, an athlete, a movie star, or a television character. Sometimes a child may simply choose a name that is not her own. A new name brings a new status in the peer group. A new name brings a new perception of self.

Children easily assume the roles that accompany the name. Three-year-old Sally was playing with a group of kindergarten and first grade children in her mother's Sunday School class. The topic for the day was names. Each of the older children was given a choice of a Biblical name and told to act out what that person might be like. Abraham was, of course, the father of the group. Tabitha was a gazelle. Jonah was a dove. Isaac was full of laughter. Leah was a wild cow. Terah was a goat. Noah "took a break" from hard work (Genesis 5:29). Tamar was a palm tree. When it was Sally's turn her mother asked what name she would like to be called (thinking that Sally would choose "Jesus," meaning "Savior"). Sally thought for a moment and said, "I will be called 'Boss-and-Leader.' " And, in a very determined fashion, Sally proceeded to arrange the other children/characters into an order for an elaborate story she shared for the next several minutes. Sally, once just "Teacher's little girl," became "Boss-and-Leader" for the entire class. A new name brings new status.

The Old Testament lesson for today describes new names and a new status for a people in the midst of very disheartening and discouraging circumstances.

After fifty years of captivity in Babylonia, Jewish exiles had returned to their homeland expecting only times of great joy and celebration. Instead they faced an enormous task of rebuilding. The walls of the fortress city of Jerusalem lay scattered in broken pieces. The once magnificent Temple was in ruins. Any possibility for restoration appeared to be hopeless. Instead of a renewed national status similar to that achieved under the kingship of David and Solomon, the nation was in helpless disarray. Instead of the Lord's leadership in renewal, it appeared to the people that they had been abandoned. The name of once proud Judah became *Azubah*, or "Forsaken." The name of the chosen covenant people became *Shemamah*, or "Desolate."

It was indeed a time of great stress and tension within the post-exilic community. One can almost hear the taunts hurled at the prophet. "You prophets of the Lord promised a glorious return. You said the blind and deaf and crippled and women and children would be gathered in celebration. You said that the darkness will be turned to light and the rough places would be made smooth. You said that this was all part of the Lord's plan to redeem us and to restore our rightful place among the nations" (Isaiah 40-55, see especially chapters 42 and 43). "Well, now what, prophet? We are nothing but a forsaken people living in a desolate land. Where is God in all this now?"

Most of the people may have given up. But Isaiah did not. "For Zion's sake I will not keep silent, and for Jerusalem's sake I will not rest," he proclaims (v. 1). Isaiah promises that he will continue to declare the renewal of the Lord until the people perceive it for themselves. Here is the central focus of today's text. To demonstrate the reality of this new status in the Lord, Isaiah says to them, "You shall be called by a new name which the mouth of the Lord will give" (v. 2).

Remember Sally? "Teacher's-Little-Girl" became "Boss-and-Leader." A new name brought new status. A new name brought a new self-understanding and a fresh, new perspective. The same would be true for the nation of Judah. The same would be true for its people.

Azubah and *Shemamah* became *Hephizabah* and *Beulah*. The formerly forsaken people and their desolated nation became "Delight of the Lord" — "Married" and no longer standing alone in ruins (v. 4). New names, new status, new perceptions of relationship; new gifts from God.

Isaiah reminds the people that just as a young man chooses a maiden for a lifelong relationship of love in marriage, "so shall your builder [the Lord] marry you" (v. 5a). "Just as the bridegroom finds delight in his bride so shall your God rejoice over you" (v. 5b).

Here was a message that the people could understand. It may have been difficult to grasp how the Lord could take delight in them as they found themselves in the midst of a shattered and scattered community. However, Isaiah was describing a relationship that they could understand: the loving and joyful relationship of the wedding day. This love sees not the blemish, but only the beloved. Now the message of Isaiah came into sharper focus.

Perhaps Zion was indeed God's beloved. Perhaps the Lord had not forgotten them after all. They really were not alone in this mess. They truly were loved and the recipients of the Lord's delight.

There is also a powerful message here for us. When everything goes wrong that can go wrong in our own lives, our perspective becomes that of the "forsaken" by others and by God. Our home, our land, our relationships become "desolate" wastelands. There is no warmth. Only the frigid chill of rejection remains. The Lord's promises seem to be intended for someone else.

During a terrible cold spell in January of 1994, the city of Chicago experienced a temperature of 42 degrees below zero Fahrenheit, with a windchill factor approaching minus 75 degrees. Mrs. Victoria Moryn, a 91-year-old immigrant from Poland, was living alone in an unheated apartment. When a neighbor called to check on Mrs. Moryn and could not get a response, she called the police. When the police arrived, they discovered Mrs. Moryn on her knees. Her feet and ankles were frozen to the floor, literally encased in a one-inch thick layer of ice. At first, the police on the scene thought that she was dead. However, when a policewoman placed her hand on Mrs. Moryn's shoulder, Mrs. Moryn shivered and began a loud and repeated chant in Polish. An interpreter said that it was a prayer: "O God, help me." Mrs. Moryn was taken to a hospital and successfully treated for hypothermia, frostbite, and fluctuating blood pressure.

Few of us have ever suffered that severely from the cold. Nevertheless, we have all had times when we felt alone, forgotten, and abandoned by everybody — including God. We have experienced times when it seemed as if we had been "left out in the cold," suffering from a pain or heartache that kept getting worse. Each one of us has experienced times when it seemed as if the world had named us "forsaken" or "desolate."

Listen again to the words of Isaiah as you remember the Victoria Moryns around you and as you remember your own times of hopelessness. "You shall no more be termed *forsaken*, and your land shall no more be termed *desolate*" (v. 4). "You shall be called by a new name" (v. 2). "You shall be a crown of beauty in the hand of the Lord" (v. 3).

Yes, Victoria, there is a God of promise, and your God rejoices over you (v. 5). Just as the Lord named the children of Israel "My Delight," so has your God taken delight in you; and, indeed, in all of God's baptized children. Remember, God has given us a new name, "Child of God," when we were baptized into Christ Jesus.

On the cross, Christ has destroyed the power of the binding chains of abandonment, desolation, and sin. Christ has died that we might be called by a new name and receive a new status: forgiven sinners — children of God — the delight of the Lord.

Anything But Trivial

Epiphany 3 *Nehemiah 8:1-3, 5-6, 8-10*

Have you noticed how the Super Bowl becomes the major focus of attention in America during this time of year? The media is full of elaborate analysis of each football team as the championship game approaches. "Up close and personal" anecdotes of players, owners, and fans become major topics of conversation. Hundreds of millions of advertising dollars are invested in one game. Millions of people around the world gather around television sets to watch the game. Inevitably, the Super Bowl is one of the top ten rated programs of the entire year. The identity of fans becomes closely tied to the success of a particular team. Emotional well-being becomes dependent upon the outcome of a game. Losing a game becomes losing at life. Winning a game means winning in life. It's incredible, and yet, a short time afterward, the outcome of the game, and even the names of the participating teams, are forgotten by all but the most dedicated football fan. Who played in Super Bowl Eleven? Who won? Who lost? Name six players. Where was the game played? Soon the results of each Super Bowl have little more significance than providing answers in a game of Trivial Pursuit.

In today's lesson in Nehemiah we also see that the attention of an entire nation is focused on a major celebration. People from towns throughout Israel have gathered in one place, the water gate outside the Temple at Jerusalem (7:73). It was the seventh month,

Tishri (our September/October). They were here for a month-long series of celebrations that commemorated events that had defined their identity as a people of God. The celebrations began with the blowing of trumpets to call the people to remember the many saving deeds of the Lord.

During the seventh month was the Day of Atonement, the only day of the year when the high priest entered the most holy place of the Temple, spilling the blood of a sacrificial animal upon the mercy seat of the Lord (Leviticus 16 and 18). The people were purged from their collective sin and guilt. God's forgiveness was assured. This celebration was followed by the Feast of Tabernacles, an agricultural harvest festival of ingathering and rejoicing. It served as a reminder of God's deliverance from bondage in Egypt and the long journey through the wilderness to the promised land (Leviticus 23). Also during the seventh month the foundations were laid for the new Temple, which had been destroyed by Babylonian armies a century before (Ezra 3). These events in the seventh month were anything but trivial. They were remembered, celebrated, and shared in great detail, passed on from generation to generation. These events described both who and whose they were as God's people.

What events define your identity as a child of God? What experiences come to mind as you remember God's presence in your own life? In the life of your congregation?

Most of us are like the Hebrew people in our text. We recall turning points and times of crisis; times when we were helpless in the face of overwhelming circumstances. It was here when we experienced renewal and strength from the Lord. God's abiding love and guidance restored hope and enhanced our faith.

On July 24, during the great floods of 1992, the Missouri River north of Rockport, Illinois, blew a 400-foot hole through a levee. High winds drove water across thousands of acres of rich bottomland. Paul Tiemeyer was unable to move all of his corn, so he built an earthen dam around eight huge storage bins. However, the wind and water had turned the area into a vast inland sea. Waves poured over the dam and the wet corn expanded, exploding the metal bins and turning Tiemeyer's 1992 profits into mud.

The broken bins became a powerful symbol of human weakness and frailty against overwhelming forces. Paul Tiemeyer saw his labor of thirty years turn into mud. Looking back on that tragedy, he acknowledges that he became even closer to his family and neighbors and even more dependent upon God for strength. His faith grew. In a television interview he stated, "This is humbling. It's like I've worked all my life for nothing. I could be bitter, but I'm not. God is present and has given us the strength to go on."

At one level, Tiemeyer's identity was shattered. At the level of faith, his relationship with God was strengthened. The closer a problem is to our sense of identity, the more pain we experience, the more difficult it is to resolve, the more we need to rely on others for support, and the more dependent we are upon God's presence.

Each of us has our own memories of major losses. Each of us has experienced times of helplessness and hopelessness. Each of us has faced problems that appeared to be overwhelming, shattering our perception of who and whose we are. God in Christ is present during those times, giving us the courage to continue and to grow in renewed relationship. God did not abandon Paul Tiemeyer. God did not abandon the people of Israel. God does not abandon us.

This passage in Nehemiah is a powerful message of that very fact. During this period in history, the exiled Jews had returned from a fifty-year captivity in Babylonia. While there, faithful Jews gathered regularly to read and study the law of the Lord. It was these gatherings that helped preserve their unique identity as God's people even as they dwelt in the midst of a nation that worshiped pagan deities (Ezekiel 33:30f). When they returned home, they found the Temple in ruins and a general disinterest in reviving the very practices of the faith which united them in their identity as God's people.

Interest in rebuilding the city walls and restoring the Temple was low at best. Religious observances were slack; most of the inhabitants who remained in Judah during the exile could not even read or speak Hebrew anymore. Even if they were at all interested in the books of God's law, they could not understand their contents. Complaining and open resistance were frequent. This was an enormous threat to their identity.

During the middle of the fifth century B.C., Nehemiah was appointed governor. His task was to organize the vast rebuilding project and to carry out needed social reforms. Ezra's task was to rekindle the spiritual identity of a discouraged people.

Outside the water gate of the Temple the trumpets have sounded. The people have gathered, on the first day of this festival month. Standing at a lectern high above the people, Ezra begins to unfold what it means to live in community as the people of God, as he reads from the book of the law of Moses.

Remember that the law was written in Hebrew, no longer the language of most in attendance. So Ezra, along with Nehemiah and other Levites, clearly interpreted its meaning so that all could understand (v. 8): "And the ears of the people were attentive to the book of the law" (v. 3). The text states that they were all standing as they listened from the early morning to midday — about five hours, so this is even more remarkable. And Ezra only read portions of the law. Imagine yourself standing attentively for five hours listening to the reading of a scripture lesson. Even the Super Bowl doesn't last that long. And we view it from comfortable couches.

The people heard what was required to live as God's children applied to their own disheartening circumstances. They recognized their sin and were overcome with grief. They had failed the Lord and their heritage. They had not held fast to the very foundation of their identity and they wept.

It's painful to see ourselves as the Lord sees us, sinners who have fallen short, who have missed the mark ... again. Guilt hurts. Shame eats away at our very souls. But God loved the children of Israel gathered for the reading of the law. God's law brought tears to their eyes, grief to their hearts, and their knees to the ground. God's love raised them to forgiveness and joy. "Do not mourn or weep, for this day is holy to the Lord," declares Nehemiah (v. 9), "for the joy of the Lord is your strength" (v. 10).

We too are in bondage to sin and cannot free ourselves. But, sound the trumpets! Gather around the table! Splash in the bath of baptism, the gate to new life! God's law brings us to our knees, but God's forgiving love in Jesus Christ has raised us to celebrate the feast of victory. "For the joy of the Lord is our strength." And that is anything but trivial. That is the way and the truth and the life that lasts forever.

Dabar Adonai

Epiphany 4 *Jeremiah 1:4-10*

Twenty-five young teenagers are sitting at their desks in the classroom, minds focused on anything and everything except the complex algebra problem that their teacher is writing on the board. Suddenly, their reverie is broken by the word of the teacher: "I need a volunteer to come to the board and solve this simple binomial equation." Immediately, students become deeply involved with books under their desks. Pencils suddenly drop to the floor. Eyes become engrossed on a page, any page, in textbooks. No one dares look at the teacher. "Jerry, what about you?" asks the teacher. "I know you can do it."

Jerry's heart sinks to the bottom of his new high-top shoes. "Why me?" he thinks. "I can't do this. I'll be humiliated in front of everybody. I can't do this. That teacher has it in for me for no reason." Jerry rapidly sorts through his mental file of excuses: bad back, flu, torn hamstring muscle, chalk allergy, dentist appointment. None seem appropriate. Jerry slowly drags himself to the board. "Come on, Jerry. I'll be up here with you," encourages his teacher. "We'll go through this together." Jerry picks up the chalk. His mind goes blank. Poor Jerry.

We know that sinking feeling all too well. Each of us has been challenged to accomplish a task that seemed to require more of us than we thought we were able to give. Each of us has a prepared list of reasonable excuses for just such occasions. Each of us, like Jerry, remembers times in which refusal was not an option.

This is precisely what happened to another young boy, Jeremiah, about 627 B.C. in a small town just three miles northeast of Jerusalem. It was not the words of an algebra teacher that startled Jeremiah. It was the word of the Lord, in Hebrew *Dabar Adonai*. It was not a call to solve a complex math problem that Jeremiah resisted. It was a call to be a prophet to nations in great political, military, and religious turmoil (v. 4). It was not a call to stay in the classroom. It was a call to "go wherever I send you and speak whatever I command you" (v. 7). The Lord did not ask Jeremiah to perform a relatively easy task based on a previous homework assignment. The Lord asked Jeremiah to shatter the complacency of an entire people, "to break down, to destroy, and to overthrow" (v. 10), and while incurring the wrath of both his peers and government leaders, "to build and to plant" seeds of renewal and hope. This surely was an impossible mission, a mission that would definitely lead to rejection, beatings, and banishment. In other words, Jeremiah saw himself to be in serious trouble.

Poor Jeremiah. He lived in tumultuous and troubled times of upheaval. Sudden and violent pendulum swings were occurring on the international scene. Once-powerful Assyria to the northwest had become overextended in its vast empire. Egypt to the south was regaining its military strength. Babylonia to the northeast was beginning to flex its military muscles. And here was tiny Judah and its capital Jerusalem, right in the middle of these behemoths, struggling to survive the certain cataclysm that was on the horizon.

Judah's leaders attempted all sorts of political treaties. The religious leaders even incorporated the worship of Assyrian and Babylonian gods into temple worship of the Lord. And now God was calling young Jeremiah to speak the word of the Lord in the midst of this chaos. Poor Jeremiah. He tried the best excuse in his repertoire to get out of this awesome request: "Ah, Lord God, I don't know how to speak, for I am only a boy" (v. 6).

But the word of the Lord, *Dabar Adonai*, came to Jeremiah. This phrase, *Dabar Adonai*, is not merely a static stringing together of sounds. When you read this phrase in the Old Testament, especially in Jeremiah, the word of the Lord is a powerful, active, dynamic force. *Dabar Adonai*, the vital power of the Lord, came to Jeremiah, moving him to accept a new task and a new relationship which he was reluctant to assume. It was this word of the Lord that continued to be a driving force for Jeremiah throughout his forty-year ministry. There are more than fifty references to *Dabar Adonai* in the book of Jeremiah. For Jeremiah, for us, the word of the Lord moves, challenges, supports, and compels. It permeates our existence. It envelopes us and nourishes us in everlasting relationship.

Notice how the Lord reminds Jeremiah of a loving relationship that began even before birth. "Before I formed you in the womb I knew you, and before you were born I consecrated you" (v. 5). Here, "knew" in the biblical sense describes a deep and profoundly intimate relationship of love. Before Jeremiah was born, God took the initiative in beginning a loving relationship with him. God set apart Jeremiah for a holy mission, and the word of the Lord was the force that would see that to its accomplishment.

We also have been chosen in and for a deep, intimate relationship with God, from birth (Psalm 139:13-16). We also have been set apart at baptism; launched by the word of the Lord on a holy mission. Jesus told his disciples, and he tells us, "You did not choose me, I chose you, that you should go and bear fruit" (John 15:16). The word of the Lord takes initiative in our lives, too.

Fear and excuses don't work very well when the word of the Lord has come upon us. They surely didn't work with Jeremiah. You see, Jeremiah was not to be alone in his holy mission. Neither are we. Are you afraid of rejection and suffering? "Be not afraid ... for I am with you to deliver you, says the Lord" (v. 8). Are you anxious and uncertain about what you might say or do? The Lord touched Jeremiah's mouth and said, "See, I have put my words into your mouth" (v. 9). The dynamic, vital power of the Lord was with Jeremiah. That power of the Word of God is with us as well.

It was not easy, even then. Throughout his entire ministry Jeremiah wrestled mightily with his fear and perceived weakness. Jeremiah's anxiety often came into conflict with his prophetic mission. His heartrending struggles with the Lord are described in chapters 9, 12, 15, and 20. Yet, in pouring out his inner turmoil to the Lord, he found renewal and strength. The word of the Lord did not desert him. Jeremiah was never on his own. Neither are we. The word of the Lord is also with us.

Relying only upon our own insights and initiative, we are bound to experience confusion and helplessness. Admiral William T. "Bull" Halsey was an Allied commander in the Pacific during the Second World War. He had a reputation for devising ingenious battle plans, often waking from a sound sleep to dictate them to his aide. Admiral Halsey often remarked that this dialogue served to bring him fully awake and resulted in precise and detailed plans. On one particular night, his aide was absent and gave the admiral a pencil and note pad so that he could jot down his ideas for himself. The next morning, when he awoke, Admiral Halsey eagerly looked at his notepad, anticipating the discovery of a solution to a particularly complex problem of naval logistics. Instead, he saw, in his own handwriting the phrase, "the skin is mightier than the banana." Needless to say, this plan was never implemented.

Left on our own, without continuing dialogue with the word of the Lord, we, too, are in hopeless confusion. "Be not afraid ... I am with you to deliver you, says the Lord" (v. 8).

A young woman was packing for her first year at a distant university. Until her very last day at home, she appeared to be eager to venture out on her own. Then, as the last suitcase was loaded into the car, tears came to her eyes and she threw herself into the arms of her parents. "All right, I admit it. I'm scared, too. I might not make it. I'll miss you." Her parents, who were also in tears by this time, presented their daughter with a plaque on which these words were engraved: "The word of God will never lead you where the love of God cannot keep you." That plaque remains prominently displayed in her law office today. "Do not be afraid ... I am with you to deliver you, says the Lord" (v. 8).

God has delivered us from confusion and hopelessness. In Jesus Christ, the word of the Lord has entered our lives. In and through the suffering, death and resurrection of Jesus Christ the word of the Lord has indeed come to us with dynamic, vital, forgiving power. Do not be afraid to embark on a holy mission. The Lord is with you.

Seeing With New Eyes

Epiphany 5   *Isaiah 6:1-8 (9-13)*

John Newton was the captain of a ship carrying captured men and women from Africa to become slaves in America during the mid-eighteenth century. He gave little thought to the enormous suffering experienced by his human cargo as they were torn from home and families and herded below decks of his ship. He gave little thought to the magnitude of the sin against God and humanity in which he was a willing participant. Until that day. As he watched his captive passengers share their meager food supplies and comfort one another, and as he heard them sing songs of their homeland, Newton's very soul was in distress. Overcome by guilt, Newton suddenly saw himself with new eyes. He realized that it was he and not his human cargo that was in bondage. It was he, not those in chains below deck, who could not free himself from the chains of slavery. He knew that he was doomed. Only by God's grace in Jesus Christ could he find forgiveness.

    Of course, Newton did not "find" Christ. It was Christ who found him. It was the crucified and risen Christ who broke his chains of bondage to sin. It was the Spirit of Christ who brought Newton to his knees. It was the Spirit of Christ who led him to stop carrying human cargo and to speak out against the sin of human slavery. And it was the spirit of Christ who led Newton to respond by writing the words to a hymn that touches all of us, "Amazing Grace." Newton's words resound in our hearts: "I once was lost, but now am found; was blind, but now I see." John Newton, touched by the spirit of God, began to see himself and the world with new eyes.

Isaiah had a similar experience 2,700 years ago during a worship service in the Jerusalem Temple. The nation of Judah was approaching a crisis point in its existence. The mighty Assyrian juggernaut was conquering every smaller nation in its path. Directly on the northern borders of Judah, northern Israel was about to fall to the Assyrian onslaught. Judah itself was paying tribute to Assyria in a desperate attempt to prevent its own destruction. Social corruption and religious apathy were rampant. Political leadership was in disarray. Finally, King Uzziah, the symbolic representative of the rule of the Lord, had just died.

The very identity of the Hebrews as the people of God was in jeopardy. Indeed, the entire nation had reached a major turning point. Was the foundation of their identity in the Lord and the Lord's promise? Or was it to be placed in frantic protection payments, shaky foreign alliances, and unjust exploitation of the poor? Isaiah came to the very place where identity is shaped, nurtured, and affirmed. Isaiah, in the midst of crisis times, came to worship the Lord.

Here is a powerful message for us as well. We also are living in difficult and challenging times in which the very core of our identity as the baptized people of the Lord is challenged daily. Many label these times as the post-Christian era, for now the church is rarely perceived as the social and spiritual center of life in the community. On any given Sunday, there are nearly twice as many church members absent from worship as there are in the pews. The number of unchurched or "underchurched" persons is rapidly overcoming the number of the baptized in many areas of our nation. There is a growing number of the "sentimentally religious," who find ultimate meaning in a variety of new age beliefs and gatherings.

A recent survey of Presbyterian baby boomers indicated that there was little difference in the beliefs of persons in the two largest categories: "moderately active in any congregation" (29%), and "uninvolved, but religious" (21%). That's one half of those Presbyterians born after 1946. There's little evidence to indicate that these findings are much different in other large Protestant denominations. In this nation we are also seeing the arrival of traditional religions to which we used to send missionaries overseas. For example, the number of Muslims in the United States is nearly equal to the number of Episcopalians. Currently, there are as many mosques in our country as there are congregations in the Evangelical Lutheran Church in America. These are indeed challenging times in which we live. As in the era of Isaiah, we are at a significant turning point in the church. And the real crisis in the church is spiritual, not organizational; biblical, not financial, theological, not numerical. The real crisis in the church today is not different from the crisis Isaiah faced in Judah. The real crisis is a crisis of identity. Who are we? Whose are we? What is God calling us to do about it?

G.K. Chesterton once remarked that when people stop believing in God, they do not believe in nothing, they believe in anything.

Isaiah saw a confused and troubled nation at risk of abandoning its identity rooted in the Lord. He saw a nation ready to believe in anything that might bring meaning and stability. Then Isaiah worshiped in the Temple. It was here that Isaiah began to "see with new eyes" the power of the Lord in the midst of a dangerous turning point in his life and the life of his nation. It was at worship in the Temple of the Lord where Isaiah's identity was reaffirmed, and his challenge to mission was proclaimed. It was at worship where Isaiah clearly heard the Lord's challenge, "Whom shall I send, and who will go for us?" It was at worship where Isaiah responded, "Here am I; send me" (v. 8).

Certainly, Isaiah had been in a temple worship service before. It is possible that he might even have been a priest himself. However, on this day the time was right for him to see the familiar sights with new eyes, and to hear the oft-repeated words with new ears. The time was right for Isaiah to understand his own identity with a new heart.

The winged half-human, half-animal-like seraphim towered above the ark of the covenant, the throne of the Lord, as guardians of the Temple. They had been there since the Temple was built under King Solomon more than 100 years before. The majestic voices of the massed choirs had echoed throughout the sanctuary in countless previous liturgies. The burning coals generating the swirling smoke of incense were a common sight to Isaiah. However, now the time was right. Now, at a turning point of his life, Isaiah, like John Newton some 2,500 years later, knew that God was speaking directly to him. Isaiah heard the magnificent choral anthem resounding throughout the sanctuary: "Holy, holy, holy is the Lord of hosts; the whole earth is full of his glory" (v. 3).

Trembling in fear, overcome by a new awareness of God's tremendous power and his own sinful nature, Isaiah knew that no one could stand before the holy God (Exodus 33:18f). Isaiah confessed, "Woe is me! I am lost; for I am a man of unclean lips and I dwell in the midst of a people of unclean lips" (v. 5). Isaiah's painful confession was heard by the Lord. "Your guilt is taken away and your sin is forgiven" (v. 7). Cleansed by God's forgiving act, Isaiah was ready for an invitation to mission. The Lord asked, "Whom shall I send, who will go for us?" (v. 8).

Do you see the pattern here? Are you beginning to see with new eyes? During the crises and challenges of our lives, when the very core of who we are is threatened, we find stability and strength in the familiar words and symbols of worship, in the presence of the Lord. Here is where we see with new eyes and hear with new ears the awesome power of the Lord and our own dreadful weakness. Here is where we gather to hear the saving words, "This is my body, given for you. This is my blood, shed for you." Here is where we hear the good news: Christ has died on the cross for you. Your sins are forgiven. Go and bear fruit. Go forth in mission.

Have you ever seen those three-dimensional pictures that appear to be a random pattern of colorful geometric designs? Within this pattern is a clear, computer-generated image. In order to see it, you must relax your eyes and cease your effort to focus on a specific pattern. Your must "look through" the picture. Soon the image, a building, a landscape, or even a picture of Jesus, pops into view. You begin to "see with new eyes" what was there all the time.

This is what happened to Isaiah. This is what happens to us as we face the confusing anxieties of life. When we look at our lives through the lens of Christ, the ordinary suddenly becomes the sacred. The mysterious suddenly becomes the awesome. Routine participation in worship suddenly becomes a vital and dynamic response: "Here I am; send me."

Allow the Holy Spirit of God to touch your lips, your eyes, your heart, as you gather in the name of Christ. Place on hold your own attempts to find meaning. Let the Holy Spirit of God transform your vision of who and whose you are. As you begin to see the cross of Christ with new eyes, you too will respond with Isaiah, "Here am I; send me!"

Roots Near The River

Epiphany 6 *Jeremiah 17:5-10*

There is a cartoon on the door of a pastor's office that pictures a man with a noose around his neck, standing on a pile of self-help books. The message is clear. None of the suggestions in these books were effective in offering any guidance that would bring a solution to his problems or a promise of hope in his anxiety. Nothing he could do for himself would reduce his desperation.

Now some psychological insights are definitely important for our mental well-being. However, without connection to the forgiving and redeeming mercy of the Lord, they can leave us empty, living an "almost-but-not-quite" existence. Something is still missing.

This is the human condition Jeremiah address in today's Old Testament lesson. In the four verses of the chapter which precede our text, Jeremiah describes the self-help attempts of the people of Judah. They had sought meaning in the accumulation of personal wealth and in the pursuit of a lifestyle of accumulation. Does that also sound like a portrayal of values in our society today? Does it appear as if contemporary values are rooted more in lifestyle and less in the Gospel of Jesus Christ? Does it seem to you that for many the cross has become merely an ornament worn around the neck like a wardrobe accessory?

If so, do not be hasty about pointing fingers "out there" beyond the church doors. We must also look closely at our own priorities. Remember what happens when we point at someone else? Only one finger is directed at the sin of others while three point directly at our own hearts. Perhaps the words of the Lord to the people of Judah might also be intended for us. "Your wealth and all your treasures I will give for spoil as the price of your sin throughout all your territory" (v. 3).

Jeremiah saw that Judah's self-help attempts openly reflected the attitudes within their hearts. Their feeble acts of worship were symptoms of empty lives. These did not escape the Lord's attention. "The sin of Judah is written with an iron pen; with a diamond point it is engraved on the tablet of their hearts, and on the horns of their altars" (v. 1).

God would not forget their sin. God does not forget ours, either. Instead, in Jesus Christ, God does something better. God forgives. God blesses those who put their trust in the Lord rather than in a lifestyle of accumulation (v. 7).

In a series of short proverbs, Jeremiah contrasts the lifestyles of the godless and the godly person. The godless are "those who trust in mere mortals and make mere flesh their strength" (v. 5). This is also an accurate description of those who rely on the latest self-help fad to help them cope with the problems of the day. Their hearts turn away from the Lord, the true source of strength.

When challenges occur in their lives, they will be like thirsty shrubs in a waterless desert of salt. They will be unable to see when any relief does come (v. 6).

When we allow ourselves to seek meaning and guidance only on our own efforts, our eyes become clouded. Our perceptions become unclear and untrustworthy. Life looks just as hopeless as it does for the man in the cartoon. We see only what our deepest values reflect, that to which we have focused our attention in the past.

An interesting experiment in perception was conducted in a university laboratory several years ago. A group of graduate students were shown a series of computer-generated faces. Without informing the students that these faces were only computer creations, the scientists identified each face as that of a faculty member in another university who was judged by students to be either fair and caring or unfair and uncaring. Neither were the student volunteers told that the only significant difference between the faces was the distance the computer placed between eyes and mouth. The scientists labeled those with a larger distance between eyes and mouth as "unfair"; those with a smaller distance as "fair." Of course, this had nothing to do with fact. These were merely computer creations.

Next the students were asked to look at another series of faces which, supposedly, were those of candidates for faculty positions at their own university. This time the students were told to share their perception of potentially fair and unfair professors. You can easily guess the results. With an amazingly high percentage of accuracy, the "unfair and uncaring" faces selected had a greater distance between eyes and mouth than did the "fair and caring."

Is it any wonder that so many of us, as Jeremiah says, place our trust in mere mortals and allow our own past perception to deceive us? The graduate students placed their unquestioning trust in their own understanding.

Sin is like that. Living and trusting only in ourselves is like "living in the parched places of the desert, in an uninhabited salt land" (v. 6) — empty, dry, and full of anxiety.

Now, on the other hand, Jeremiah describes godly persons as those whose trust is in the Lord and not limited to human perceptions (v. 7). They are like fruitful trees, whose roots are near the river (v. 8a). These are not overcome by the scorching heat of life's pressures. They are not overwhelmed by an apparent absence of quick and easy self-help solutions in times of great stress. They remain nourished and well watered. Their lives continue to bear fruit in faithful service (v. 8b).

Left to our own plans and perceptions we are unable to see lasting meaning and hope in life. Too easily we grasp at any straw for life support. Inevitably, we are disappointed. By our own reason and strength we cannot completely trust in the Lord. No matter how hard we try, our will is not always one with the will of God. "The heart (will) is devious above all else," says Jeremiah. "It is perverse — who can understand it?" (v. 9). The apostle Paul states it differently. "I do not understand my own actions. For I do not do what I want, but I do the very thing that I hate" (Romans 7:15).

So then, what hope do we have if even Paul cannot help himself? Like the godly person described by Jeremiah, we need roots near the river — the river of the water of life in Jesus Christ; the river of the water of baptism.

Paul continues: "Wretched man that I am! Who will rescue me from this body of death? Thanks be to God through Jesus Christ our Lord" (Romans 7:24-25).

It is the cross of Christ that expands our perception of reality. When you are overcome by the pressures and anxieties of daily living, when you feel burdened by a heavy load of sin, look to the cross through the lens of faith.

This is precisely how God looks at you, through a holy lens that takes the form of the cross of the beloved son, Jesus Christ. Through Christ your roots are in the river. In Christ, splash in its living waters.

Who's In Charge Here, Anyway?

Epiphany 7 **Genesis 45:3-11, 15**

At age seventeen, Joseph was a spoiled brat and something of a tattletale. In order to understand the full impact of today's text, we must remember that fact. Chapter 37 of Genesis describes this in vivid detail. As the youngest of many children, and born late in his father's life, Joseph became Jacob's favorite. And Jacob did nothing to disguise it either. While Jacob's other sons wore the typical knee-length sleeveless tunics, Jacob made his "favorite" son a colorful, long and luxurious robe, with full sleeves. Joseph was known to further alienate his siblings by bringing Jacob bad reports of their shepherding work. Around home Joseph often taunted his brothers even more by sharing his dreams in which they all bowed down to him.

Is it any wonder that Joseph was not at all popular with his brothers? It's not at all surprising to read that Joseph's brothers could not bring themselves to speak any kind words to him at all. Finally the conflict reached the point of no return. Jacob sent Joseph to check up on his brothers, who were tending the flocks near Shechem, a few days' journey from home.

When his brothers saw Joseph approaching, they plotted revenge. Who could blame them? Joseph had been nothing but a source of trouble for them since the day he was born. They did all the hard work. They were faithful to their father, too. Yet Joseph received the gifts and the love that was rightfully, justly, theirs. So they plotted. After deciding not to kill him, they came up with a plan to strip Joseph of his robe of luxury and throw him into an empty cistern used for gathering rainwater.

Eventually, when a caravan on its way to Egypt passed by, Joseph's brothers sold him to the traders for twenty pieces of silver.

Joseph, the spoiled brat, would no longer trouble them. They sprinkled goat's blood on Joseph's robe and returned it to a grieving father, speculating that Joseph must have been killed by a wild animal.

Two wrongs never make a right. Joseph certainly was a spoiled tattletale. His brothers had good reason to be angry. But one sin is never canceled by another even more grievous than the first. Joseph's brothers knew that. We know that. We are in bondage to sin and cannot free ourselves. We sin by what we have done and by what we have left undone. Getting even may feel good at the time, but invariably more trouble results.

Joseph, the brat, became Joseph, the prime minister of Egypt. The rich and successful brothers became hopeless victims of a terrible famine which forced the entire family to flee for survival. And their flight for food took them directly to Egypt, and Joseph.

We cannot suppress the pain of broken relationships forever. We cannot escape the increasing, energy-draining pressure that results from living in conflict. We cannot escape our desperate need for the nourishment and wholeness that comes through being reconciled with our sisters and brothers in the Lord. Soon this pressure builds and builds until it makes little difference what the original cause for separation was. The pain is too great. Forgiveness and renewal are our only hope for alleviating our distress. Someone must take the first step. Someone — anyone — even the most injured party, must take some initiative to restore the relationship.

And this is precisely what God has done and is doing in Jesus Christ. This is part of God's plan. Not ours. Regardless of our own futile attempts to justify our actions, God is in charge, not us.

Our text today describes what happens in relationships when God takes initiative. The long famine had driven Joseph's family to Egypt in order to sustain their lives. Settling in a narrow strip of grazing land, Goshen, they found themselves near the Pharaoh's capital and soon came face to face with Joseph himself. Their spoiled little brother was now the second most powerful person in Egypt. The teenage tattletale was now in charge of their food supply. Oops!

Through Joseph, God took the initiative in reconciling a long-standing and bitter conflict. When Joseph first met his brothers, they did not recognize him, but Joseph immediately knew them. He was so overcome with emotion that he excused himself and began to weep (Genesis 43:30). After further conversation with them about their situation and the welfare of Jacob, their aging father, Joseph sent everyone else from the room and began to cry "so loudly that the Egyptians heard it and the household of Pharaoh heard it" (45:2).

The pain of broken relationships grows until it permeates our existence. It expands until it controls our emotions. It becomes so toxic that it spills over and touches everybody around us.

However, it doesn't have to be like that. Joseph had a perfect opportunity to make his brothers suffer deeply for selling him to a bunch of wandering nomads and telling everyone that he was dead. Revenge could have been so sweet for Joseph. After all, he was in power now, not his brothers. His dreams had come true. Theirs were shattered. What a perfect opportunity for gloating. The spoiled brat could have turned into an even more obnoxious adult. But God was in charge here. Someone had to take the first step to affirm that.

After his tears subsided, Joseph called his brothers close to him and told them who he was. Through Joseph, God brought an end to a long and bitter conflict. Joseph said to his brothers, "Do not be distressed or angry with yourselves because you sold me here; for God sent me before you to preserve life" (v. 5).

Evil exists. Conflicts happen, even in the best of families, even in the most faithful congregations. We often have a desperate need to be right, all the time. We draw lines in the sand and dare anyone to cross them. That's human nature. Unfortunately, that's also sin. It hurts. It tears apart. It renders us helpless. It condemns.

There is an old story about two brothers who seemed to be at each other's throats since birth. The older continually picked on his younger sibling and blamed him for every misfortune the family experienced. After a four-year military separation, the two brothers went into business together. Their fights continued and, if anything, the older brother was even more critical and hostile. Yet the younger brother remained diligent in their business and faithful in their relationship. Everyone marveled at this saintly behavior.

One day a terrible accident ended both of their lives. Saint Peter was waiting patiently for the younger brother's arrival at the heavenly gates. Finally when he did not appear, Saint Peter ventured down into the fiery place of torment. "You belong in heaven," said Saint Peter. "Come up with all the saints." Up to his neck in slime and stench, the younger brother replied, "No. I choose to remain here."

Puzzled, Saint Peter urged him even more fervently. "Please come with me. You have been faithful. A place has been made ready for you. Why won't you take your rightful place in eternity?"

By this time the burning slime had nearly covered the chin of the younger brother. Lifting his face to Saint Peter, he shouted, "If I come with you, I will have to stop standing on my brother's head."

We have all found ourselves caught up to our chins in hot, bubbling, boiling conflict. We have all felt the gut-wrenching anxiety of discord and dissension. We have all tried in vain to control for ourselves that which seems to be unending chaos. But God is in charge. We are not. God's plan is forgiveness and reconciliation through Jesus Christ. God takes initiative. In the midst of chaos, God brings order to preserve life. In the midst of an apparently hopeless conflict, God invites us to a transforming opportunity for love and forgiveness.

Joseph allowed himself to be an agent of the Lord in restoring peace with his family. "God sent me before you to preserve for you a remnant on earth" (v. 7). He continues, "So it was not you who sent me here, but God" (v. 8).

God used this reunited family to continue the promise made to Abraham (Genesis 12:2-5) that from his children would come a great nation. God used this nation to be the birthplace of a King who promised to reconcile the world, even you and me, unto

Himself. God did not allow the sin of the brothers or the spoiled behavior of the young Joseph to divert this divine plan.

Families fight. Christians quarrel. In some congregations conflicts become so severe that members refuse to kneel at the altar with sisters and brothers who disagree with them. Others are given the silent treatment. Still others are the victims of gossip and innuendo. Chaos continues. Sin abounds.

"And Joseph kissed his brothers and wept upon them; and after that his brothers talked with him" (v. 15).

Someone has to be a Joseph here. God is in charge here. Not you. Not me. We must "stop standing on our brother's head." God calls us to reach out with the open arms of forgiveness. God asks us to put aside our desires to get even. God calls us to allow peace to begin in our own hearts. God calls us to love as we have been loved in Christ. God calls us to forgive as we have been forgiven by Christ.

Why not here? Why not now?

Looking Back; Moving Forward

The Transfiguration Of The Lord   ***Exodus 34:29-35***
(Last Sunday After The Epiphany)

A young college student was searching for a summer job to help defray the rising cost of his education. He finally found one with the State Transportation Department, where he was given the task of hand-painting the white lines in the middle of the road.

The supervisor informed him that she expected him to complete ten miles per week, and took him to the job site.

"Place your paint buckets right here," she instructed, "and begin painting white lines from this spot."

The first day went very well. The student covered four miles of lonely highway. The supervisor was pleased. The next day he was only able to extend the white line by one-half mile. Day three ended with merely a quarter mile painted. Day four was even worse. The student was able to add only one hundred feet to his white line. Finally, at the end of the fifth and last day of the work week, the exhausted and disheveled student sadly informed his supervisor that he had barely completed ten additional yards of white line.

"What happened to you?" she asked. "You started out with four miles and then you could not even complete one mile in the next four days combined."

"Well," the student replied, "I put down my supplies and began exactly where you told me. The first day did go smoothly. But, each day, I kept getting farther and farther from my paint bucket."

Here is a problem for most Christians. If we are not careful, each day we also keep putting more distance between ourselves and our crucial resource on the journey of life; our perception of the continuing power and presence of Jesus Christ. If we are not careful, we limit our awareness of Christ's presence to spiritual mountaintop experiences in our past. Christ's presence becomes restricted to a "feeling" of spiritual joy. If we don't have that "feeling," then we think that Christ must not be with us anymore. We must do something to find the feeling again. We want to "find Christ" even though Christ is always walking with us wherever we might be. We desperately try to "find Christ" when it is we, not he, who are lost.

Moses' face shone with the glory of God only when he descended from Mount Sinai holding the two tablets of the covenant (v. 29). When Moses came down from the mountain, the people were confused and afraid to come near him (v. 30). He had to cover his face with a veil. The awesome demands of God's law and the reality of their sin were overwhelming. Perhaps it was only Moses who could come into the Lord's presence and survive.

Moses had to gather the trembling people to himself. Only then could Moses begin to explain the plan the Lord had for them to live in community as the people of God (vv. 31-32). It was a magnificent plan. It was a frightening plan that would guide people though the unknown terrors of the wilderness into the promised land.

It was a plan that would be both foolish and futile if the Lord had not promised to be with them throughout the journey. And so Moses instructed the people to construct the Ark of the Covenant, which was to be the throne of the Lord and the container of the commandments. It would serve as a reminder of God's continuing guidance and power on that marvelous day when they finally entered the promised land. Now the people could carry with them on their journey of promise the very presence of the Lord God.

Jesus brought the disciples down from a glorious mountaintop experience to walk with him to Jerusalem on a journey that led straight to the cross. It, too, was a frightening journey. It was a journey of suffering and hope, passion and promise, despair and joy. It is a journey that Jesus invites us to share today. The Ark of the Covenant of the Lord was carried triumphantly by the children of Israel throughout their wanderings. The cross was carried in glory by Jesus to Calvary. The cross of Christ is carried by us today in victory over the power of sin and the suffering that seek to destroy us along the way.

The shining face of Moses as he received the Lord's Commandments and the transfigured appearance of Jesus as he prayed with the Father are critical moments in the lives of the people of God. Here we see the connection of memory and hope, history and promise. Here we discover new insights into God's will; new discoveries of identity; new directions for living. Something fresh and exciting has been added.

Have you ever ridden in a canoe? You know that maintaining equilibrium in that canoe is quite precarious at times, especially when proceeding along a rapidly flowing river. Now imagine that another person is attempting to get into that canoe with you. What happens? Definitely a lot of shifting and adjusting must happen or a terribly cold dunking for everybody will be the unpleasant result.

When Moses received the tablets of the law and Jesus prayed on the mountain of transfiguration, critical shifts in the balance of meaning and direction occurred in the lives of the people of God. Things could never be the same again. New stability and transformed identity provided power to venture into an unknown and frightening future. These critical events were turning points for the children of God.

Try something. On a piece of paper draw a horizontal line from one side to the other. This is your "Life Line." Near the left end draw a short vertical line intersecting it. Write your birth date here. Somewhere near the right end, make another similar vertical line. Write today's date here. Now, in between those two dates, draw two or three additional vertical lines that intersect your life line. These represent major turning points in your life.

These lines are experiences that have greatly inspired who and whose you are today. What were they? Looking back, how was God active and pivotal in shaping you? What connections do you see between memory and hope, history and promise? What "baggage" needed to be adjusted and shifted in order to provide new stability and balance?

Look carefully at this paper. Do you notice that each turning point in your life is represented by a cross? Sometimes during the actual experience, we see only pain and confusion. Sometimes a veil seems to hide God's loving care and mercy from our eyes. And then, looking back again, from a new perspective, we see clearly the guiding presence of the Lord.

It is the awareness of Christ's real presence with us that gives us vital nourishment to face times of suffering. It is the presence of Christ that gives us courage to serve others in his name. It is Christ in our midst who gives us power to face the chaos and confusion that accompany our early pilgrimage.

Today, Transfiguration Sunday, we celebrate that glorious reality of Christ's presence with us. And, today, we prepare to begin our descent from the Christmas mountaintop to walk with Christ and the disciples on the road to Jerusalem. Today we begin our journey from the shining face of the baby in a manger to gaze at the agonized face of a Savior on the cross. Today the going gets tough. Today Christians get going. Today we look back to the mountaintop in order to walk forward in the valley, confident that the sure and certain presence of Christ is with us.

Oliver Wendell Holmes once remarked that in order to understand what is happening today or what will happen in the future we must look back. In order to find renewed strength to face a fearful present and to move forward towards an uncertain future we must look back to the mountain where the truth was gloriously revealed.

Looking back, the Hebrews could see God's presence in the shining face of Moses as he came down from the holy mountain with the commandments of the Lord in his hands. Moving forward, carrying with them the Ark of the Lord, they caught a vision of the promised land. Looking back, the disciples could see the transfigured face of Jesus as he was revealed as the intersecting point between the law of God and the prophecy of the coming Messiah. Moving forward, they began their journey with Christ to the cross. Moving forward, Peter, James and John still had a veil before their eyes. They could not see clearly beyond their fear of arrest and condemnation.

But *we* can see clearly. We can see the cross and empty tomb as shining beacons of light that urge us onward. We can move forward with vigor. Christ has removed the veil from our eyes. Christ has died. Christ has risen. Christ will come again. Christ, our eternal resource, walks with us in our journey, on the way.

Books In This Cycle C Series

Gospel Set
Sermons For Advent/Christmas/Epiphany
Deep Joy For A Shallow World
Richard A. Wing

Sermons For Lent/Easter
Taking The Risk Out Of Dying
Lee Griess

Sermons For Pentecost I
The Chain Of Command
Alexander H. Wales

Sermons For Pentecost II
All Stirred Up
Richard W. Patt

Sermons For Pentecost III
Good News Among The Rubble
J. Will Ormond

First Lesson Set
Sermons For Advent/Christmas/Epiphany
Where Is God In All This?
Tony Everett

Sermons For Lent/Easter
Returning To God
Douglas J. Deuel

Sermons For Pentecost I
How Long Will You Limp?
Carlyle Fielding Stewart, III

Sermons For Pentecost II
Lord, Send The Wind
James McLemore

Sermons For Pentecost III
Buying Swamp Land For God
Robert P. Hines, Jr.

www.ingramcontent.com/pod-product-compliance
Lightning Source LLC
Chambersburg PA
CBHW071734040426
42446CB00012B/2351